# PAINT YOUR HOME

A READER'S DIGEST BOOK

Published by The Reader's Digest Association Limited
Berkeley Square House
Berkeley Square
London W1X 6AB

ISBN 0 276 42295 3

This book was designed and produced by
De Agostini Editions
Interpark House
7 Down Street
London W1Y 7DS

Publishing Director: Frances Gertler
Art Director: Tim Foster
Senior Editors: Michèle Byam, Louise Tucker
Assistant Editor: Jonathan Aris
Art Editor: Paul Tilby
Illustrations: Grundy & Northedge
Photographers: Geoff Dann, Tim Imrie, Matthew Ward

Printed and bound in Spain by Cayfosa, Barcelona

**Warning**
All do-it-yourself activities involve a
degree of risk. Skills, materials, tools
and site conditions vary widely. Although
the editors have made every effort to
ensure accuracy, the reader remains
responsible for the selection and use of
tools, materials and methods. Always
obey local codes and laws, follow
manufacturers' instructions and observe
safety precautions.

# PAINT YOUR HOME

## SKILLS, TECHNIQUES AND TRICKS OF THE TRADE FOR SUCCESSFUL INTERIOR PAINTING

**PUBLISHED BY**
THE READER'S DIGEST ASSOCIATION LIMITED
LONDON • NEW YORK • SYDNEY • MONTREAL

# Contents

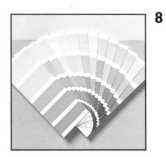
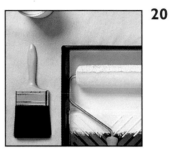

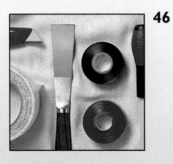
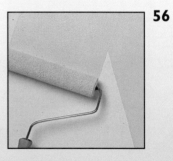

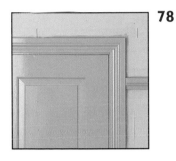

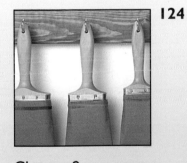

# Introduction

**W**hy paint your home? As the proverb has it, "home is where the heart is", but it is also where we live, eat, sleep, raise families, entertain friends and relax. Because of this, your home's appearance can profoundly effect your whole outlook on life; and painting your home can play a key role in beautifying your living space. A lick of paint can transform a home; and a truly integrated approach can achieve just the right mood, and give you something to enjoy every day.

So why *not* paint your own home? Invariably, budding do-it-your-selfers are told: "This is a job for professionals only!", or "It is so time-consuming". Neither is true. Far from being a chore, painting can be fun, and beginners can master the basic skills and experience that enjoyment for themselves.

How often have you had an idea for a painting project, but did not know where or how to begin? Now *Paint Your Home* guides you through the first planning stages and on towards learning the proper techniques of painting. It shows you how to judge the quality of tools and equipment. By working at your own pace, you will soon build up confidence. Above all, you will really feel in control.

The book is structured like a painting project. There are sections on tools and materials, plus easy-to-follow painting instructions accompanied by clear, precise illustrations, and tips on cleaning up. Each chapter covers a different aspect of painting and builds on previous information. By reading the chapters in sequence you will be sure not to miss important parts of the project, or any of the tips and shortcuts that are scattered throughout the text. All of this will help you to do a better job, cut your working time, and even save you money.

The book opens with a guide to selecting the right colours for your project. This straightforward, practical approach helps you to avoid making expensive mistakes. It shows you how to combine colours by explaining how the colour wheel works, and tells you how you can use colour for effect, and to highlight or hide features in a room.

By choosing suitable paints and tools for each project, you can be assured of an ideal finish. The book also answers technical queries. For example, it describes what substances go into a tin of paint, and it explains the differences between the various types of paint on the market. The right tools can make your project much easier and quicker, so *Paint Your Home* suggests what tools and equipment you need, and how to use and look after them properly. Painting techniques and preparation form the heart of *Paint Your Home*. Using clear instructions and illustrations, it shows you the right way to hold and use brushes, rollers and other applicators. Once you have mastered this, you can tackle any painting project with confidence.

To help you achieve professional results, *Paint Your Home* shows you how to prepare the room before you begin and how to make ready surfaces, such as walls and ceilings, and fixtures and fittings, such as kitchen cabinets. Step-by-step instructions guide you through the painting tasks themselves.

At the end of every job there is, inevitably, some cleaning up to be done. *Paint Your Home* dispenses useful advice on how to clean and store tools and equipment. It describes methods for the disposal of used paint and solvents, and offers guidance on the safe storage of unused materials.

*Paint Your Home* makes paint and painting easy to understand. It guides you through every stage of the process. By following the clear instructions and advice, you will enjoy the rewarding experience of painting your own home successfully.

**FRANCIS DONEGAN**

# CHAPTER I
# COLOUR

The paint colours that you choose for the walls, ceiling and floor in each room of your home make an important decorating statement. Paint colours not only reflect your personal tastes, they also establish the style and character of your home. Because colours affect how you feel when you are in a room, they may be used to create moods. They can also be used to influence how you and others perceive the size and shape of a room.

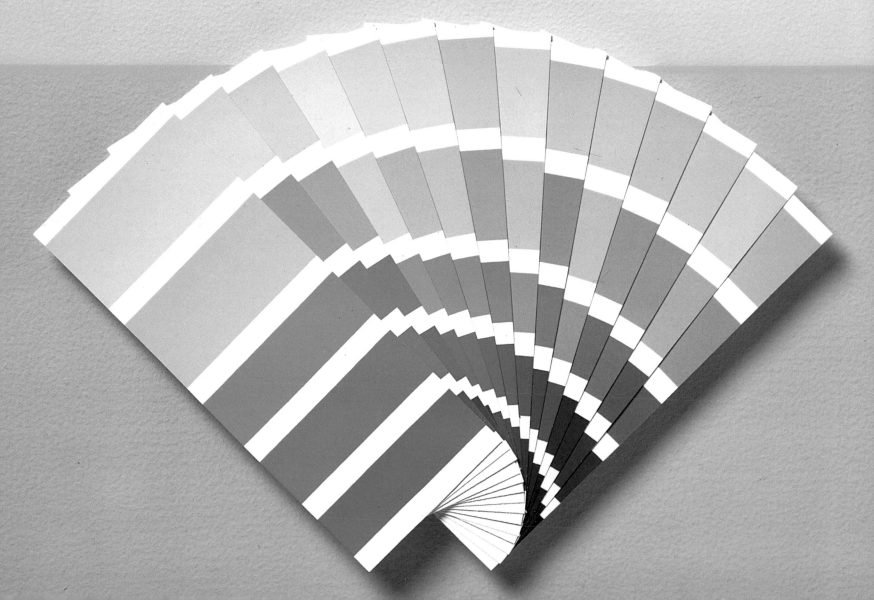

# Choosing colour

There are thousands of paint colours to choose from, and each year manufacturers introduce dozens more. Begin the process of choosing your colours by deciding which you like best. Then consider what the room will be used for and what overall effect you wish to create. Paint colour can be used to alter the spatial proportions of a room, to highlight features and to detract from flaws. Other important factors to consider include the room's lighting and existing furnishings. This chapter will help you to combine your personal colour preferences with the needs of the space to be painted. This knowledge will enable you to avoid mistakes. The main considerations are:

**Understanding colour** It is important to understand how colours are created and how they work with one another. The colour wheel is a useful device for understanding colour, and it can help to make selecting colour combinations easier. The colour wheel is also useful for matching paints with furnishings, woodwork and other elements in the room.

**Creating an effect** Consider what the room will be used for when you decide on the effect you wish to create. Rooms can evoke different moods: the feeling of a cosy bedroom is different from the mood of a large family room. The paint colours you select will help to create the mood. Also, colours can change the perceived dimensions of a space, making small rooms feel larger or large spaces more intimate.

**Taking cues from the room** You can use paint to hide unsightly features in a room, such as a run of pipes. By the same token, you can use colour to highlight an architectural element or other feature. The light in a room also plays a part in colour selection. Be sure to consider both natural and artificial light sources.

**Dealing with your furnishings** The colours of walls, ceilings and floors cannot be considered in isolation. Rooms contain furniture, fittings, carpets and pictures, and the colours you select should blend with whatever is in the room.

**Planning your work** Before you start a painting project, make sure that you have the correct colour and quantity of paint. You should estimate how long the job will take and whether you will need to hire a contractor for some of the work.

## COLOUR TRENDS

Paint colours fall in and out of favour, as other products do. Fortunately, paint-colour cycles usually last for seven to ten years rather than the one-year or two-year cycles of fashion colours. When changes do occur, they tend to be gradual. So, the colours you choose for your walls today will not be out-of-date next year.

The current trend is for warm colours, inspired by nature. Even cool colours, such as blues and greens, are being made warmer with the addition of yellow. The colours tend to be pale, especially when used over large surfaces. You can enliven a pale, warm scheme by including accents in brighter colours.

# Understanding colour

The human eye can distinguish between about 10 million different colours. All are derived from just three primary colours – red, blue and yellow. The primary colours are blended in different combinations, with white or black added to the mix. Primary colours cannot be created by mixing other colours.

**The colour wheel** The colour wheel is a simple device that can help you to choose colours and combinations of colours. The wheel features the three primary colours positioned equidistantly round the circle. Between each of these are the secondary colours – orange, green and violet – created by mixing the two primary colours on either side. Tertiary colours are created by mixing a secondary colour with a primary colour. Colours can be mixed with one another in almost limitless combinations to create new colours. Tints are created by adding white to colours. Adding black creates darker versions of colours, called shades.

The position of colours on the colour wheel can help you to combine paint colours in the home. Complementary colours, which lie directly opposite each other on the wheel, and related colours, which are positioned side by side on the wheel, usually make the most successful combinations.

## COLOUR TERMS

Three words are often used when describing colours: hue, value and intensity. These terms help to describe paint colours more precisely.

- **Hue** is the name of the family to which a colour belongs. For example, the hue of a ruby-coloured vase is red.

- **Value** describes the relative lightness or darkness of a colour. Light colours have a higher value than dark colours. For example, lemon yellow has a higher value than deep gold. Tone is a term that is often used interchangeably with value.

- **Intensity** describes how saturated with pigment a colour is – in fact, intensity is often called saturation. A highly saturated, or intense, colour will seem bright, rather than subdued.

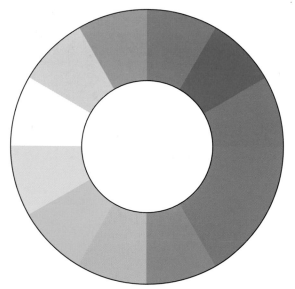

**The colour wheel**
This simple colour wheel shows the three primary colours, the three secondary colours and the six tertiary colours. By mixing different combinations of the colours on the wheel, and adding black or white, it is possible to produce every other colour.

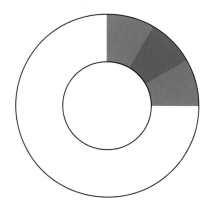

**Related colours**
Related colours are positioned next to one another on the colour wheel. As they are made by mixing elements of each colour, related colours blend together and do not clash. Any group of related colours used in a room will create a harmonious scheme.

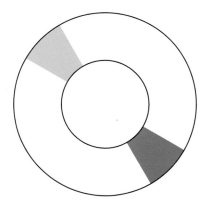

**Complementary colours**
Complementary colours lie directly opposite each other on the colour wheel. When two complementary colours are used together, each will provide a contrast for the other. Complementary colours can be used to create attractive, dramatic colour schemes.

**The properties of colours** As you work with complementary and related colours, take into account other principles that affect how colours work. Consider the different qualities of warm and cool colours, light and dark colours and neutral colours before choosing a colour scheme.

## Warm and cool colours

Warm colours are grouped together on the colour wheel – they contain elements of yellow and red. Warm colours can make a surface appear to advance and a room seem small and intimate. Cool colours contain elements of blue and green, making a surface appear to recede from the viewer, and a room seem larger. The room on the right is painted in a warm, peach colour and it seems more intimate and smaller than the cool, blue-green room on the far right.

## Light and dark colours

A light-coloured surface reflects more light than a dark-coloured surface. Consequently, rooms that are painted in a light colour will appear more open and larger than they really are. Even a warm colour can have this effect if it contains enough white. Dark colours absorb light, define spaces and make a room appear smaller. So, the dark blue room on the far right seems smaller than the pale blue room on the right.

## Neutral colours

Neutral colours – black, white and grey – do not appear on the colour wheel. Other colours with a great deal of white or black, such as beige and cream, are also called neutrals. Neutral colours can provide the backdrop for other colours, or they can be used alone, as in the room shown here, to create a harmonious scheme.

### COLOUR MIXING TIPS

- Colours appear to be more intense when set on a white or near-white background.
- Dark colours look even darker when placed near light colours.
- Complementary colours look more intense when used next to each other.

# Creating an effect

Colours can be used to create moods and to alter our perceptions of space. Consider what the room will be used for when deciding on the colour scheme. You can combine colours to create the required effect following the principles of complementary and related colours, warm and cool colours and light and dark colours *(see pp.10-11)*.

**Creating a mood** As a rule, warm colours evoke a cosy, intimate mood and cool colours, a tranquil mood *(see p.11)*. However, you can combine colours to create other effects. For example, red details in a blue room will make the cool, tranquil room feel warmer and both colours will appear more vibrant. The lightness and darkness of colours can affect mood, too. Deep yellow will produce a more intimate effect than pale lemon will.

**Creating spatial effects** One of the most amazing aspects of colour is the way it can visually change the shape and size of a room. If a room is painted with a light colour, the walls will seem to recede, creating the impression of a larger space. Cool colours *(see p.11)* will achieve the same effect. You can create the opposite effect by using dark or warm colours.

## COLOURS AND ARCHITECTURE

The architectural style of your house may help you to select paint colours. Many paint manufacturers have created colour lines to complement specific styles of architecture, such as neo-classical, Victorian or Art Deco. Others have developed paint collections that evoke the look of regional architecture, such as Mediterranean or Mexican. There are also palettes of colour that suit more generic decorating styles, such as traditional or country.

These paint collections can be helpful because they reduce thousands of colour choices to a more manageable number. All the paints in a palette share common characteristics, so, if several colours are selected from the same palette for one room, they should work well together.

## CREATING MOODS

**Cool, light, related colours**
This room is painted in shades of cool blue and blue-green, which create a relaxing, tranquil effect. The colours are light, making the walls appear to recede, so the room feels airy and open. As all the colours are related, they create a unified scheme.

**Warm, dark, complementary colours**
This room appears warm and intimate because the deep-brick-coloured walls are dark and contain red. The walls appear to advance into the room. Sea-green woodwork complements the brick-coloured walls and adds impact to the scheme.

## CREATING SPATIAL EFFECTS

### Unifying interconnecting rooms
You can create an impression of unity and spaciousness in your home by painting interconnecting rooms in related colours. These will lead the eye from one room to the next, and produce a harmonious effect.

### Different walls, different colours
Make a long, narrow room seem wider by painting the narrower walls in a warm, dark colour, so that they appear to advance. The long walls will appear to recede if you paint them in cool, pale colours.

### Making a ceiling appear higher
A wall divided by a picture rail provides an interesting challenge. Here, the ceiling and the wall above the rail are a lighter colour than the wall under the rail giving an illusion of spaciousness and a high ceiling.

### Making a ceiling appear lower
This ceiling and the wall above the picture rail are painted a darker colour than the wall under the rail. This makes the ceiling appear to be lower and creates a more intimate effect.

# Highlighting features and hiding faults

Paint colour can enhance or camouflage elements in a room. Before you start to paint, consider which features should have impact, and which need concealing.

**Highlighting features** To enhance an architectural feature, such as a cornice or a window frame, give it a paint treatment different from the surrounding area. You could use complementary colours (*see p.10*). These lie directly opposite each other on the colour wheel and, when placed side by side, tend to make each other stand out. An alternative strategy is to create contrast with light and dark colours. For example, dark green will stand out on a pale yellow background even though the two colours are near each other on the colour wheel.

**Hiding faults** To help conceal a fault, such as an ugly radiator or pipes, make it blend in with the background. One way to do this is to camouflage the fault by painting it the same colour as the wall that surrounds it. Another method is to use a matt paint sheen rather than a shiny finish.

## HIDING FAULTS

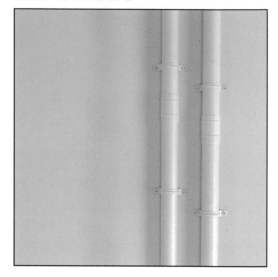

**Pipes**
These pipes have been painted the same colour as the surrounding wall area. This helps to make them appear less noticeable.

## HIGHLIGHTING FEATURES

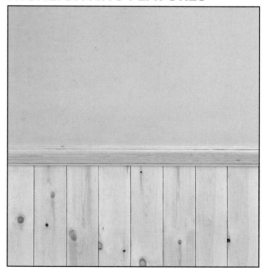

**Walls and woodwork**
Wainscoting can be an attractive feature. Here, the wood has been left unpainted and the wall has been painted in lilac. The lilac complements the colour of the wood and draws attention to it.

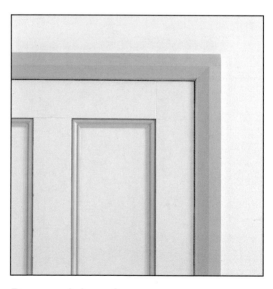

**Door and door frame**
This panelled door has been painted in two related colours, which emphasise the panels, but retain a feeling of unity. To harmonise with the door, the door frame has been painted in the same colours.

**Cornices**
A cornice can be a stunning architectural feature. This one has been painted in a lighter colour and shinier finish than the surrounding wall, which make the moulding stand out.

# The effect of light

The type and intensity of light can change the appearance of a paint colour. When you are selecting colours, consider the natural light in the room, and the type of artificial lights that you will use.

**Natural light**  The quality of natural light in a room will affect paint colours. For example, bright colours seem brighter in direct sunlight. The natural light will be governed by the time of day, the season and the direction in which the window faces. Generally, natural light at noon has a blue cast, and an orange cast at sunrise and sunset. The time of sunrise and sunset alters with the seasons and light is brighter in summer than winter. The direction in which a window faces will determine when the room receives most natural light and whether it is direct or indirect.

**Artificial light**  The main types of artificial lights used in homes are incandescent, fluorescent and halogen lights. Incandescent light has a yellow cast, slightly deeper than that of sunlight. It is best with dark, warm colours. Fluorescent light contains blue, is best with bright colours and white, and is often used in kitchens and bathrooms. Halogen light gives a strong white light that defines bold colours, but can cause muted hues to appear washed out.

## HOW LIGHT AFFECTS COLOURS

**How natural light affects colours**
The quality of natural light changes through the day. This picture shows a room at noon when the natural light is at its brightest. The pale walls appear to have a slightly blue cast. A south-facing window will receive direct light brighter than the indirect light received by a north-facing window.

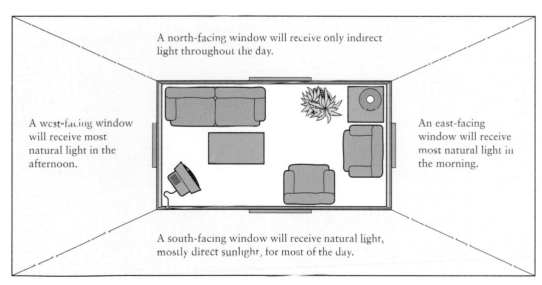

A north-facing window will receive only indirect light throughout the day.

A west-facing window will receive most natural light in the afternoon.

An east-facing window will receive most natural light in the morning.

A south-facing window will receive natural light, mostly direct sunlight, for most of the day.

**Get your bearings**
The direction in which a window faces governs when a room receives natural light and the type of light it receives. Light will shine through different windows at different times, as the illustration above shows.

**How artificial light affects colours**
At night, all the light in a room will come from artificial sources. The light from incandescent bulbs produces a yellow cast, which makes the room seem warmer.

# Using existing furnishings

When selecting paint colours, it is very important to consider the dominant colours in the existing furnishings, or in those which you plan to add to the room. Just as the colours of the walls and the woodwork should harmonise, so should the painted surfaces, the furniture, pictures, curtains and floor coverings. Often, new furniture or carpeting calls for repainting the room.

Do you want your furniture to stand out or blend in with the colours of the walls and the woodwork? Photographs, or works of art which you intend to hang on the wall will also govern your choice of colour. A busy, primary-coloured art print will lose impact when hung on a brightly coloured wall, but it will stand out against a neutral one.

Consider any other objects in the room which will have to harmonise with the paint colours you have chosen. Houseplants will add green, and natural wood will add brown to the colour scheme of a room. Natural-wood furniture and a wooden floor will create a feeling of warmth in a room.

**Paint and wallpaper**
Paint has been used with wallpaper in this room. The wallpaper under the dado rail has pale-peach and deep-peach stripes and pale peach has been selected for the paint above the rail. This combination creates a well-balanced scheme of related colours.

**Brightly patterned sofa**
This bright sofa in the complementary colours of blue and terracotta is the focal point of the room. The colours work well together because the walls have been painted the same deep terracotta as one of the less-dominant colours in the sofa fabric.

**Pale-patterned rug and curtains**
The pale greens in the rug and curtains are all related colours. The walls have been painted a pale pink that complements the pale green. This creates a harmonious scheme, which draws attention to the rug and the curtains.

**Houseplants in a warm-coloured room**
The houseplants in this room 'cool down' the red walls. Green complements red, and each colour seems more vibrant when placed next to the other. The sisal flooring provides a neutral ground for the strong colour of the walls.

# Planning your painting project

Before beginning your painting project, make sure that you have planned each stage of the work. This involves buying the paint, making sure that you have set aside enough time to complete the job and hiring a contractor, if necessary.

**Buying the right colour** You can begin your quest for the perfect paint colour by taking a sample of the colour in any medium – it could be a swatch of fabric from your favourite curtains, a cutting from a magazine or chips taken from a damaged wall painted in a colour you want to replicate. The sample will help you either to find a match in a paint manufacturer's range of standard colours or to have a paint custom-blended.

The most common method of selecting paint colours is by using manufacturers' paint swatches. These are strips of paper, each with a different shade of a single colour. You can use them to check which colour most closely matches your sample. Also, you can test which colours will work best with the existing colours in your home. Try several manufacturers' ranges, because the colours may vary in each collection. If you don't find the colour you want in any range, you can have a paint custom-blended.

To request a custom-blended paint, use your sample or find a paint swatch close to the colour you want, and take it to your supplier. Some suppliers use computers to analyse colours and can blend the paint to match the sample. It is difficult to ensure that, once applied, the custom-blended paint will match the sample exactly. Paint and fabric colours look different because of their finishes. If you try to match a paint colour to a fabric sample, the painted surface may look slightly different. Also, textures on walls, or variations in paint sheen, may lead to a mismatch between the original sample and the end result. Buy a small tin of paint first, and try the colour on a test patch of the material you will be painting. Allow it to dry and study the effect for a week, in different parts of the room and in different lighting conditions.

## COMPUTER MATCHING

Many paint suppliers use computers to help them create custom-blended colours. The process is simple. You provide the computer operator with a matt colour sample, usually at least 12mm (½in) in diameter. The sample is placed in a device attached to the computer. The computer analyses the colour on the sample and breaks it down into its primary-colour components. It then produces a recipe for the paint.

Depending on how complex the colour is and how good the sample is, the computer should produce a list of ingredients for mixing exactly the right colour. Buy a small amount and test the colour on sample boards. If the colour is not suitable, the shop can alter the formula slightly and blend a new colour.

This service is provided free at some shops (it is included in the price of the custom-blended paint). Other retailers charge a minimal fee. The custom-blended paint will cost more than paint chosen from a manufacturer's range, but you are more likely to obtain the colour you want.

## WHITE PAINT

Buying white paint isn't as straightforward as you may think. Most manufacturers offer a range of whites with names such as Antique White, Linen White, Lilac White and, even, Off-White. None of these is pure white paint. They all contain small amounts of pigment. When buying paint, make sure that the white you choose is the shade you want.

## BUYING THE RIGHT QUANTITY

To estimate the amount of paint you will need, calculate the areas of the surfaces to be painted in each room. To measure the area of a ceiling, multiply the length of the room by the width. To calculate the area of a wall, multiply the length by the height. Calculate the area of all the walls by adding their separate areas together. Be sure to include the additional areas of any alcoves. Then, calculate the area of each window and door by mutiplying its height by its width. Subtract the total area of all windows and doors from the total area of the walls. To calculate the area of mouldings, multiply the height by the length. For narrow trim, measure the sides and tops of windows and doors and add the totals together. Next, multiply the area to be painted by the number of coats of paint you intend to apply. Divide the result by the surface area that one tin of paint will cover. Most tins state a coverage rate of about 15m² (161ft²) per litre for smooth interior walls. However, it is best to estimate that one tin will cover only about 12m² (129ft²), then you will have a little paint left over for repairs or corrections.

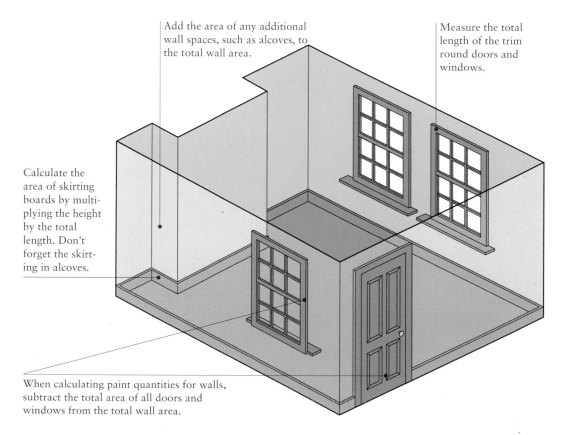

Add the area of any additional wall spaces, such as alcoves, to the total wall area.

Measure the total length of the trim round doors and windows.

Calculate the area of skirting boards by multiplying the height by the total length. Don't forget the skirting in alcoves.

When calculating paint quantities for walls, subtract the total area of all doors and windows from the total wall area.

**Calculating the surface areas of walls**
Most rooms are not perfect rectangles. Measure the dimensions of each section of wall separately and add them together to find the area. You may have more than four wall areas to add together.

## A QUESTION OF TIME

Home improvement projects always take longer than you expect, and painting is no exception. Professional painters can cover at least 40 square metres (430 square feet) of wall surface with a roller in one hour. You may equal that rate in the first hour, but you are likely to tire and slow down. Preparatory work, like moving furniture, will make the job take even longer.

Below is a practical schedule for painting a 6 x 3 metre (20 x 10 foot) living room. Adapt the schedule for your project:

**Day 1** Buy your materials and supplies. If you are planning to start the project on a specific day, buy your materials a day or two before the work will begin. Finding the right tools and paint may take longer than expected.

**Day 2** Do all the preparatory work. This will include moving furniture, putting down dust sheets, and so on. These are time-consuming tasks that should be planned adequately.

**Day 3** Paint in the right order. Plan your sequence of work. If you start early, you may be able to apply a second coat of water-based paint on the same day that you applied the first.

## HIRING A CONTRACTOR

Although you should be able to paint your home yourself, you may wish to hire a professional for a particularly difficult area, or if time is at a premium. A professional should do a good job and complete it quickly. Cost is the major drawback to hiring a contractor. As much as 80% of the cost of a typical paint project can be attributed to labour charges.

### WHAT SHOULD BE IN EVERY CONTRACT

A contract between you and a contractor should contain the following:

- The contractor's name, business address and telephone number.
- The cost of the project.
- The scope of the project.
- Material specifications, such as the type of paint.
- Start and completion dates of the project.
- Penalty clause for work not completed on time (most contractors will resist this, but try to include it).
- The deposit the contractor requires.
- A payment schedule. (Don't pay the entire bill before the job is done. Hold back 5–10% as a final payment to be paid on completion, once you are happy with the work.)

### CHECKLIST FOR HIRING A CONTRACTOR

- Gather names of potential contractors. Painters are listed in the Yellow Pages and they often advertise in local newspapers. Check with other people who have had similar work done in your area. Recommendations are generally more valuable than advertisements.
- Discuss the project with three or four different contractors. Ask them how they will prepare the surfaces before painting, the types of paint they recommend and how long the project will take. You should ask to see the company's Certificate of Insurance, and check the details.
- Ask for references. Contact the referees and ask questions about the contractor. Ask if the final cost was the same as the original estimate, and if he, or she, was punctual and cleaned up properly.
- Ask for estimates. Supply each contractor with the same specifications and ask for an estimate for the job.
- Make a selection. When making your final decision, consider the estimates, references and also whether you think you will get along with the contractor.
- Draw up a contract.

**CHAPTER 2**

# MATERIALS AND TOOLS

One way to ensure the success of any painting project is to use good-quality materials and tools. There are hundreds of paints available; this chapter will enable you to select the one that will work best on the surface you want to cover and protect. Complement premium paints by using the correct tools. They will make your work easier, and will help you to achieve the best results.

# What's in paint?

Paints can be divided into two broad categories: water-based paints, such as acrylic and vinyl paints, and oil-based paints. Within each group there are many different products. Some, such as primers and topcoats, are designed for specific tasks and others, called speciality paints, are designed for specific conditions. Most paints contain the same basic ingredients – solvents, binders, pigments and additives.

Although all paints are made from these same ingredients, the quality of the raw materials and the formulas used to blend them together make one paint different from another. For example, high-gloss paints contain a relatively high proportion of binder, which is left behind to form a protective layer on the surface when the solvent evaporates. On the other hand, matt paints, which give the dullest finish, contain a smaller amount of binder.

**Solvent** makes paint fluid and easy to apply. Water-based paints are so-called because water is the solvent used. In oil-based paints, the solvent is either a white spirit, such as benzene, or a plant derivative, such as turpentine. As paint dries on a surface, the solvent evaporates, leaving only the solids (the binder and pigments). The solvents used in paints are the same materials that are used for the cleaning up of painting equipment.

**Binder** makes paint stick to surfaces and develop a protective film. New binders are usually made from plastics. In water-based paints, the binder is usually an acrylic material or a combination of vinyl and acrylics. In oil-based paints, the binder is an oil-based product or a synthetic resin known as alkyd resin.

**Pigment** is made of finely ground particles that give paint its colour and covering ability. The particles tend to sink to the bottom of the tin, which is why it is important for paint to be shaken or stirred before it is applied to a surface. Clear varnishes are unpigmented paints.

Some pigments are better than others. Prime pigments give the paint colour and opacity. Extender pigments add bulk to the paint. Good-quality paints contain a high percentage of prime pigments.

**Additives** enhance paints. Some make the paint easier to apply, some reduce mildew; others thicken paint to reduce drips.

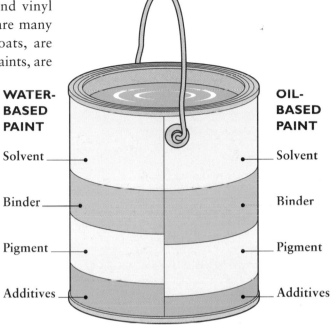

WATER-BASED PAINT

OIL-BASED PAINT

Solvent — Solvent

Binder — Binder

Pigment — Pigment

Additives — Additives

**PROFESSIONAL TIP**

Paint tin labels provide important information. They usually tell you the type of paint and whether it is oil-based or water-based, the surfaces to which the paint can be applied and how much surface it will cover. The label may also give advice on preparing the surface. Also, the label will provide safety, health and environmental information which you should read before you open the tin.

# Types of paint

While both water-based and oil-based paint can be used on interior walls and woodwork, water-based paint is preferred by most homeowners and many professional painters. There are three main reasons for this:

1  Water-based paint usually dries within a few hours. This means you can apply two coats in the same day.
2  Brushes, rollers and the painter can be cleaned with soap and water. The cleaning up of oil-based paint requires harsh chemicals, such as white spirit or turpentine.
3  Compared to oil-based paint, water-based paint is relatively free of unpleasant odours and fumes. It also contains fewer volatile organic compounds than oil-based paint (*see right*).

However, the long drying time of oil-based paint can be an advantage. It helps to produce a smooth finish, because the longer the paint stays wet, the more time it has to level out. This helps to eliminate brush marks, especially on wood.

## VOCs AND PAINTS

Volatile organic compounds (VOCs) are carbon-based chemicals, such as those found in petrol, alcohol and paint thinners. They can damage the lungs and form smog when they react with the atmosphere or sunlight. Oil-based paint contains the highest levels of VOCs, although a small amount can be found in water-based paint. Many paint manufacturers are now introducing new, less toxic, types of water-based paint, and, in time, these are likely to replace most, if not all, oil-based paints.

Use water-based paint when possible. If you must use oil-based paint, make sure the room is well-ventilated at all times. This will help disperse the fumes.

## TYPES OF PAINT

| General Types | Comments | Surfaces |
| --- | --- | --- |
| *Water-based paint* | The most widely used type of paint for walls, ceilings and woodwork; it does not normally require thinning and is easy to apply and clean up. Most painters like water-based paints because they dry within a few hours. However, some people are sensitive to their odours. | Primed wood, plasterboard and plaster. Surfaces previously painted with water-based paint. |
| *Oil-based paint* | Oil-based paint gives a durable coating. Modern oil-based paint has a synthetic resin as a binder, and it has largely replaced older-style paint which contained linseed oil. It can be cleaned off with white spirit or turpentine. | Primed wood, plasterboard and plaster. Any previously painted surface. |
| **Specific-use paints** | | |
| *Ceiling paint* | This is thicker than standard water-based paint. It gives better coverage and tends to drip less than standard paint. | Ceilings. |
| *Floor paint* | Designed to withstand the heavy wear that floors are often subjected to, they are available in both water and oil bases. Some floor paints contain epoxy additives for increased adhesion. | Wood and concrete floors. |
| *Textured paint* | This is water-based paint that contains a component such as sand or styrofoam beads, which provides a rough, stucco-like texture. It is useful for disguising flaws in walls and ceilings. | Primarily plasterboard ceilings, but may also be used on walls. |
| *Kitchen and bathroom paint* | A relatively new type of water-based paint which often contains a fungicide to deter mould. | Ceilings and walls. |
| *Paint for children's rooms* | A few manufacturers have introduced water-based paint designed for use in children's bedrooms and playrooms. This paint is easier to clean than other types of water-based paint, and it is nontoxic. | Walls, ceilings and woodwork. |

## PAINT SHEENS

It wasn't so long ago that the choice of paint sheens was fairly limited. Every painter knew that matt paint was used on walls and semigloss or high gloss was usually used on woodwork. But, since the introduction of intermediate levels of gloss, these rules have changed.

The new finishes make it easier to match the gloss of the paint with the surface to be covered. However, along with the new paints came a confusing array of new names to describe their gloss levels. Some of the descriptions you are likely to encounter, ranging from the least-glossy finish to the shiniest, are matt, low-lustre, eggshell, silk satin, soft gloss, semigloss, gloss and high gloss.

Don't be confused if you see the word enamel combined with a paint sheen, such as semigloss enamel. Enamel paints dry to an extremely hard finish, but may come in different sheens.

### Comparing paint sheens

Each level of paint sheen has different characteristics. For example, matt paint absorbs light rather than reflecting it, so it is a good choice for disguising flaws in a surface. Because the paint finish is not completely smooth, dirt will adhere to it more easily than it will to gloss paint, and it may require more frequent washing. High-gloss paint has the opposite qualities. It reflects light and appears very shiny. The finished surface is very smooth, which means it attracts very little dirt. However, because the glossiest sheens accentuate imperfections on a surface, they are rarely used to cover entire walls.

Before selecting a sheen, consider the location and condition of the surface to be painted, and how much wear it may need to withstand. Generally, you should cover walls with a matt or eggshell paint and woodwork with a semigloss or gloss.

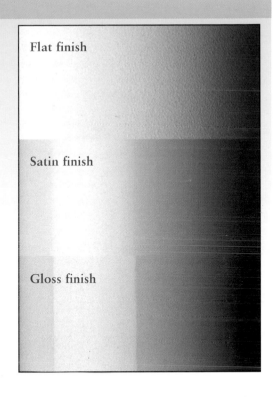

Flat finish

Satin finish

Gloss finish

## MATCHING SHEEN TO SURFACE

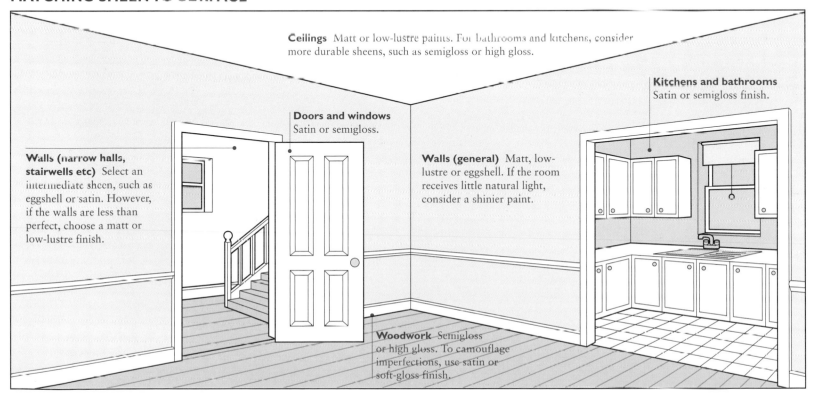

**Ceilings**  Matt or low-lustre paints. For bathrooms and kitchens, consider more durable sheens, such as semigloss or high gloss.

**Kitchens and bathrooms**  Satin or semigloss finish.

**Doors and windows**  Satin or semigloss.

**Walls (narrow halls, stairwells etc)**  Select an intermediate sheen, such as eggshell or satin. However, if the walls are less than perfect, choose a matt or low-lustre finish.

**Walls (general)**  Matt, low-lustre or eggshell. If the room receives little natural light, consider a shinier paint.

**Woodwork**  Semigloss or high gloss. To camouflage imperfections, use satin or soft-gloss finish.

# Primers

Beneath every fine finish there usually lies a specialised coat of paint – a primer – that helps to hide blemishes and bond the finish to the underlying surface. If the surface is new plasterboard, for example, an ordinary paint will simply be absorbed into the material, resulting in an uneven, splodgy finish. Wood knots that have bled through the old paint on a section of skirting board, for example, will bleed through new paint in a short time unless they are treated with knotting before the new paint is applied. Refer to the box on primers (*right*) for advice on how to select the right one. In most cases, you can use either water-based or oil-based paint over primer, but check the paint-tin label to make sure.

Most primers contain very little pigment, but they seal the surface to which they are applied and provide a good base for the top coat of paint.

Primers dry more quickly than most paints (*see p.25*). This means that you can usually prime and topcoat the same surface in one day. Primed surfaces should not be left exposed for long periods of time, as they are neither durable nor weather-resistant. If you wait too long before applying the top coat, you may need to re-apply the primer first. Check the label on the primer for recommendations on timing.

Primers are available in both water and oil bases. Most are white, but you can tint them to resemble the colour that you will be using as a topcoat, or ask your supplier to do it.

In addition to primers that are brushed or rolled on, spot primers are also available. These often contain shellac and are available in tins and aerosols. Spot primers are useful for hiding wood knots and preventing resins from bleeding through the finished surface.

## PRIMER ON PRIMERS

| Surface to be painted | Recommended primer |
|---|---|
| Unpainted plasterboard | Water-based primer. |
| Unpainted plaster | Water-based primer. |
| Unpainted wood | Oil-based or water-based primer. |
| Wood knots, other stains | Knotting. |
| Previously painted walls, ceilings, woodwork | Water-based, but choose oil-based if staining is present. |
| Repairs in plasterboard or plaster | Water-based primer. |
| Repairs in wood | Oil-based or water-based primer. |
| Masonry | Primer designed for masonry. Both oil-based and water-based available. |
| Metal | Primer for metal. Use on new metal or where rust has been removed. Special primers for rusty metal are also available. |

## SPECIALITY PAINTS

*Some paint products are designed for special uses. Read the directions carefully before using.*

| Type | Comments | Where to use it |
|---|---|---|
| Epoxy Paint | For covering nonporous surfaces, such as ceramic tiles and metal. Difficult for the amateur to apply correctly. | Nonporous materials: tile, metal, plastic. |
| Heat-Resistant Paint | Will not degrade at high temperatures. | Hearths, radiators, pipes etc. |
| Waterproofing compounds | Some water-based and all oil-based paints help to prevent condensation being absorbed into the walls and ceilings of steamy rooms such as kitchens and bathrooms. | Walls and ceilings. Good when used as a primer in bathrooms. |

# Stains and varnishes

In addition to paint, there are other types of coatings that can be used to enhance or protect the wood in your home. These include transparent finishes, such as stains, and special sheens such as varnishes.

**Stains** are designed to colour a surface, but still allow the wood grain to show through. Unlike paints, which form a protective layer on a surface, stains are absorbed into the wood, but they must be covered by a clear protective finish – a varnish.

**Varnishes** are clear finishes that form a tough coating over stains. They can also be used over painted surfaces. Like paints, they are available in both water-based and oil-based versions. Polyurethanes are the most popular varnishes, because they are easy to apply and very durable. Traditional yacht varnish is often used where a flexible gloss finish is needed. A large number of other products has been developed to meet special needs. They are available in a range of finish sheens from satin to high gloss.

**Coloured sealants** are a combination of wood stain and varnish. They are available in water-based and oil-based versions. They provide a finish that will colour and protect the wood in a single application.

**Transparent stains**
These allow most of the wood grain to show through the finish, thereby enhancing the appearance of the wood.

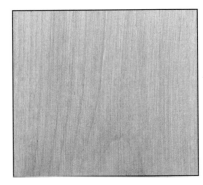

**Semi-transparent stains**
These allow some grain to show through.

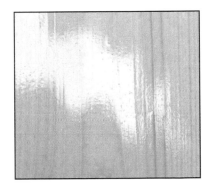

**Varnishes**
These are clear finishes that protect the surface to which they are applied. Most commonly used on stained wood, but they may also be applied over paints.

## DRYING TIMES FOR PRIMERS AND PAINTS

| Type | Typical drying time* |
|---|---|
| Water-based primer | 1–4 hours, recoat immediately. |
| Oil-based primer | 4–10 hours, recoat after 24 hours. |
| Pigmented shellac | 30 minutes to 1 hour, recoat immediately. |
| Water-based paint | 2–4 hours, recoat immediately. |
| Oil-based paint | 6–10 hours, recoat after 24 hours. |
| Water-based stain | 2–4 hours, apply protective coat after 12–24 hours. |
| Oil-based stain | 4–6 hours, apply protective coat after 24 hours. |

*\* Check label for specific drying and recoating times.*

# Brushes

Paint brushes are divided into two categories: natural-bristle brushes, which are made from animal hair, and synthetic-bristle brushes, which are made of nylon, polyester or a combination of the two. As a general rule, use a brush with synthetic bristles for water-based paints and a natural-bristle brush for oil-based paints. You can use a good-quality synthetic-bristle brush for oil-based paints, but never use natural bristles with water-based paints, as the bristles will absorb water and the brush will be ruined. Many painters believe that the best natural-bristle brushes are made from boars' hair. These are called China-bristle brushes. Nylon and polyester are equally good for synthetic-bristle brushes.

**Testing the quality of a new paint brush** Good paintbrushes have dense bristles. You should check that the metal ferrule is solid and well-attached to the handle, which can be of wood or heavy-duty plastic. The bristles of a good-quality brush are well-anchored to the handle, while those of an inferior one will come out in your hand. Set a 'bargain' brush next to a more expensive one and the difference will be clear.

| THE RIGHT BRUSH FOR THE JOB | |
| --- | --- |
| **Brush size** | **Uses** |
| 12mm (½in) | Mouldings, windows |
| 25mm (1in) | Mouldings, cutting in (p.130) |
| 50mm (2in) | Window frames, skirting boards |
| 75mm (3in) | Flush doors, walls, ceilings |
| 100mm (4in) | Walls, ceilings |

**Brushes**

The width of the bristles determines a brush's suitability for the job – the finer the brush, the more intricate the area it can be used for.

**Using new brushes**   Remove the wrapping and drag the brush back and forth across your palm, flexing the bristles slightly with your fingers. They should spring back into position when you release the pressure.  Before painting, dip the brush in the appropriate solvent (water if you are using water-based paint, white spirit for oil-based paint) and remove the excess.

**Refurbishing old brushes**   A brush that is stored properly won't need to be refurbished. However, if you neglected a favourite brush the last time you painted, follow these steps:

1   Soak the brush overnight in the appropriate solvent (*see above*). If using white spirit, keep it away from open flames.
2   Remove the paint (*below right*).
3   Shake the brush well and blot it on newspaper.
4   Test the bristles by pulling them lightly and flexing them against a hard surface. If some of the bristles are still stuck together or, even worse, if some fall out, invest in another brush.

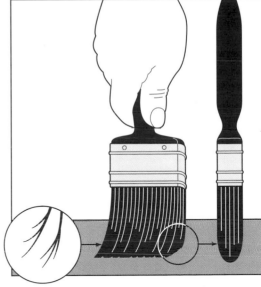

**Choosing a good-quality brush**
A good brush has long, lush bristles; cheaper ones have a large wedge inside the bristle clump to reduce bristle thickness. Bristles should be of varying lengths, forming a chiselled edge at the tip. Each should have a flagged or frayed end to apply the paint smoothly and evenly.

**Using a brush comb**
Plastic or metal brush combs and wire brushes provide one way of removing paint without damaging the bristles.

# Rollers

Rollers allow you to paint large open areas of walls, ceilings and floors quickly and efficiently. All rollers have two sections: the handle and frame, which is sometimes called the sleeve; and the hollow cylinder that holds and applies the paint. Standard roller covers are 175mm (7 inches) or 225mm (9 inches) long, although some professionals use 450 mm (18 inch) rollers and slimline covers are available for painting smaller, restricted areas.

**Using a new roller**   Remove the wrapping and smooth out the pile with your hand. Apply the appropriate solvent (*see p.126*) and rub it into the pile. Remove excess solvent by squeezing the roller with your hand. Load the roller with paint and make a few practice passes on some scrap material before tackling a wall or ceiling.

### TYPES OF ROLLER SLEEVE

| Pile length | Recommended surfaces |
| --- | --- |
| Short | Flat walls and ceilings. |
| Medium | Surfaces with small flaws and bumps. |
| Long | Textured surfaces. |

## Choosing a Roller Frame

The frame should have a sturdy wire cage which spins freely on its axle and which grips the sleeve firmly. When you squeeze the frame, the sides should spring back into position as you ease the pressure. The handle should be comfortable to hold, and may have a hollow, threaded end to fit an extension pole for painting ceilings and high areas (*p.70*).

## Roller Sleeves

Synthetic roller sleeves work well for applying water-based paints. For oil-based paints, use lamb's-wool or mohair sleeves. The core of the sleeve should be made of plastic; cardboard cores degrade quickly and will not last.

Short pile

Medium pile

Long pile

# Power rollers

These are designed to pump paint directly from the tin or from a special reservoir to the sleeve of a paint roller. Because you don't have to continually stop painting to load the roller, you can finish a job relatively quickly. However, you must keep the roller moving to avoid drips and runs.

The typical power roller kit will contain roller extensions, sleeves, a hose, a pump and a reservoir or paint-tin cover. Make sure that the hose is long enough to make using a power roller worthwhile. If the hose is too short, you will need to keep moving the paint tin or reservoir, which defeats the whole purpose of using this type of roller. Since it takes additional time to set up a power roller and to clean it at the end of the project, consider using these tools only for large projects.

# Paint pads

These tools consist of a foam plastic painting surface and a plastic handle. They can be used to apply water-based paints and water-based varnishes. Harsh solvents, such as those found in paint removers, can melt the pads.

Large paint pads allow you to work faster than you would be able to with a brush, but not as quickly as you could with a roller. However, pads are rarely used for large open areas because they tend to spread the paint too thinly, and a second coat is then required. Smaller paint pads, though, are good for narrow sections of trim, such as mullions on windows.

**Painting pads**
Common sizes of pads include: 100mm (4in) pads for large flat surfaces, 50mm (2in) pads for large areas of trim, 12mm (1/2in) pads with tapered edges for narrow areas of trim. Some larger pads can be attached to extension poles.

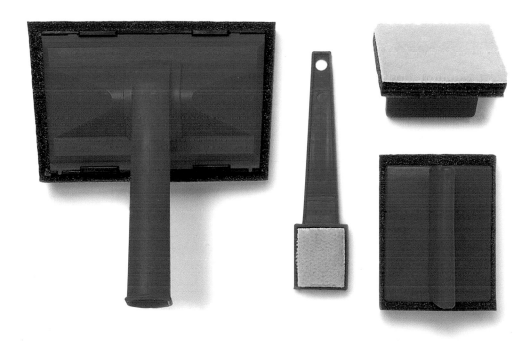

# Paint sprayers

The advantage of using a paint sprayer is that it can cover large areas quickly. There are two basic types. The paint sprayer most often sold at DIY centres and hardware shops is the airless model, which uses an electric pump to deliver the paint to the surface; the other type of paint sprayer uses compressed air to apply the paint. Newly marketed models of air sprayers – called HVLP sprayers – are less wasteful of paint. Until you are familiar with this tool, you will find spray painting the interior of a house tricky. Anything not to be painted in the room must be covered to protect it from overspray, otherwise you will need to spend a long time cleaning up. It also takes time to master the technique of applying the paint smoothly without drips or runs. Cleaning spray equipment is especially important. If it is not thoroughly cleaned, it may malfunction or not work at all when you want to use it again.

**Power spray equipment**
Sprayers that use air atomise the paint during application, while airless models create a fine mist of paint. Some models are made for specific jobs, such as painting furniture or applying water-based paint to walls.

# Solvents

As already mentioned, all paints contain some type of solvent to keep the paint liquid. Solvents are also used to make the paint thinner when necessary and for cleaning equipment (*see p.126*). Before starting to paint, some professionals like to use a little solvent on a new brush or roller to condition it.

You must always remember that, with the exception of water, all solvents are dangerous. They are flammable, irritating to the skin and respiratory passages and poisonous. Solvents should be handled and disposed of with care. Large quantities many need special handling by a local waste disposal authority (*see p.128*).

## SOLVENTS AND SAFETY

When cleaning painting tools with solvents, wear rubber gloves and eye protection. Not only are solvents flammable, their fumes can also catch fire if exposed to an open flame. Be sure to extinguish flames and work only in a well-ventilated area. Also, make sure that you store solvents in sealed containers.

## SOLVENTS AND THEIR USES

| Type of solvent | Use |
|---|---|
| *Water* | To clean brushes and rollers used with water-based paint. To remove dried drips and spills of water-based paint. To thin water-based paint. |
| *White spirit and turpentine* | To clean brushes and rollers used with oil-based paint. To remove dried drips and spills of oil-based paint. To thin oil-based paint. |
| *Brush cleaner* | To recondition equipment which is covered in dried paint. |

# Other tools

There is a number of other tools which you may find useful for your painting project. As with brushes and rollers, buy good-quality products to ensure good results.

## OTHER PAINTING TOOLS

1  **(23 litre) 5 gallon  roller bucket with roller screen**
2  **Small bucket**
3  **Paint-mixer drill attachment**
4  **Roller tray**
5  **Painting mitten**
6  **Straight edge**
7  **Aerosol paint**
8  **Brush comb**
9  **Roller extension**

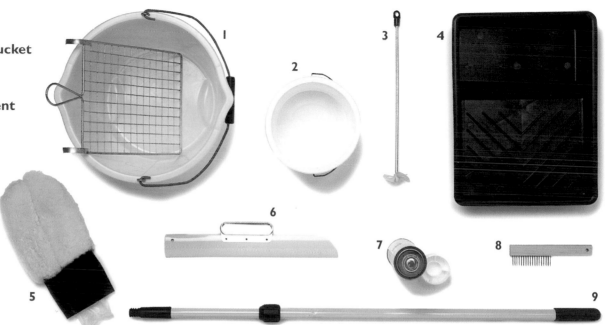

## OTHER USEFUL TOOLS

1  **Painter's tape**
2  **Plasterboard knives**
3  **Putty knife**
4  **Scoring tool**
5  **Glass fibre joint tape**
6  **Wire brush**
7  **Cutting knife**
8  **Dust sheet**
9  **Sanding block**
10  **Sandpaper**
11  **Rubber gloves**
12  **Sponge**
13  **Hook-bladed paint scraper**
14  **Flat-bladed paint scraper**

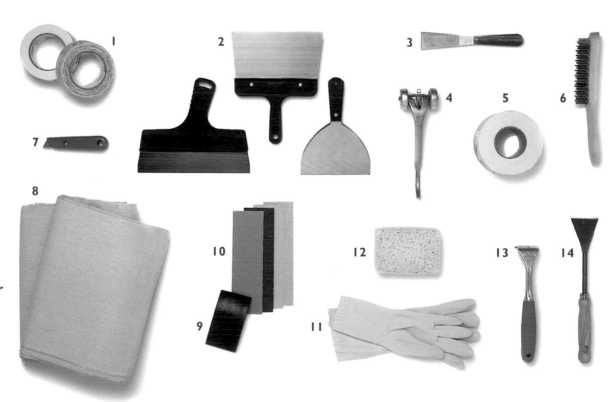

# Ladders and platforms

Good-quality ladders and the right work platform allow you to paint the tops of walls and ceilings safely and efficiently. Even if you use a roller extension for reaching high areas, you will still need a ladder or work platform for cutting in (*see p.130*) and for detail painting with a brush.

**Ladders** When shopping for a ladder, make sure it has a label that says it is made to British Standard BS 2037 (for aluminium ladders), or British Standard BS 1129 (for timber ones). These certify that the ladder meets manufacturing standards recognized by the industry. Make sure that the hinges are strong and that the ladder is steady when it is open. Nonslip pads on the feet of the ladder will help to steady it. Also make sure that the steps of the ladder are wide enough to accommodate your feet comfortably. A wooden ladder should have a metal rod fitted beneath each step for added support. Some stepladders are fitted with either a wide-top platform or a fold-out shelf that provides a safe resting place for paint tins or roller trays while you are decorating. Never stand on this platform or shelf. It is not designed to take your weight.

**Choosing a good ladder**
A good-quality stepladder should have a sturdy feel to it when you set it up in the shop. Don't rely on your own judgement alone, however; look for a label that states the load-bearing capacity of the ladder and that it is made to British safety standards.

**Work platforms** Ladders alone are insufficient for such jobs as painting stairwells and other high places. This is when you will need a work platform. A platform made of interlocking frames saves you time because you don't have to continually climb up and down and move it as you would a stepladder. You can purchase a work platform from a DIY store or paint dealer, or you can rent one from a tool-hire company. Alternatively, you can make a platform using trestles and boards, or a plank supported by two stepladders *(see below)*.

## SETTING UP A WORK PLATFORM

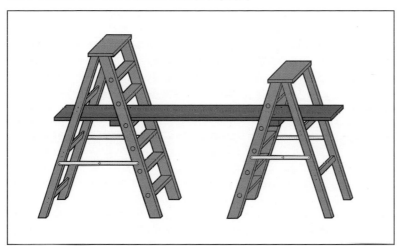

### Create a work platform between two stepladders

Two stepladders can make excellent anchors for a work platform. Make sure that the ends of the plank overlap the steps of the ladder by at least 300mm (12in). If the plank sags when you walk on it, move the ladders closer together.

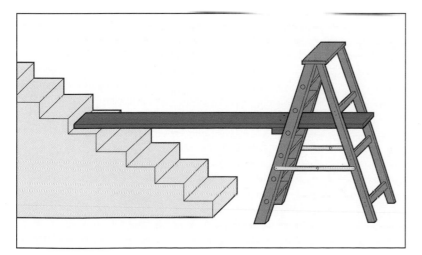

### Create a work platform between a stepladder and stairs

Stairs can be used to anchor one end of a work platform. The stair riser will help to keep the plank in place. Add a cleat to keep the plank steady. If necessary, protect the stair with an old towel.

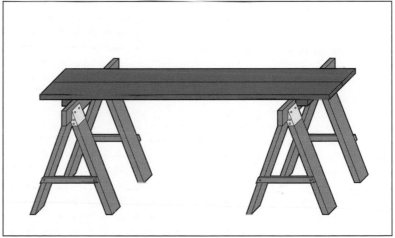

### Create a work platform between two trestles

Two trestles can be used to support a work platform. Nail horizontal braces between the legs at each end of the trestles to reinforce them. Add cleats to keep the platform from shifting while you work.

# CHAPTER 3
# PAINTING TECHNIQUES

Professional painters are good at what they do because they use special techniques that have been refined by years of practice. This chapter explains the basic painting techniques that will help you to achieve professional-looking results. It covers everything from how to prepare the paint and develop the best brush and roller techniques, to ways of solving problems you discover when the job is finished.

# Working with paint

When you start a painting project, you may be using either a new tin of paint, or a previously opened tin left over from another job. In either case (unless it is non-drip paint), stir it well to make sure that the components are properly blended, and that it is free of lumps and foreign matter.

**Use small containers** You will find it easier to work from containers smaller than the large tins that paint is usually sold in. When painting with a roller, use a roller tray; when working with a brush, use a small paint kettle. Both are lighter, easier to handle and allow you to load the roller or brush more efficiently than if the paint were in the tin. A roller tray hooks onto the paint shelf of a ladder, and a small kettle is less cumbersome than a large tin. In addition, both of these containers hold a small amount of paint that must be replenished as work progresses. This will remind you to stir the tin so that its contents do not settle while you are working. Using another container keeps the rim of the tin clean, making it easier to replace the lid at the end of the job.

Trays and kettles cost very little and are available in plastic or metal. The plastic models are best because they won't rust after you've cleaned them. If you are using an old tray or kettle, wash and dry it thoroughly before adding paint. These tools are usually stored in cellars or garages where they collect dust and dirt which, if not removed, could ruin a paint finish.

**Thinning paint** Although it is not necessary to thin paints for most jobs, some special applications, such as decorative finishes (pp.75–77), may require that the paint be thinned. Use water to thin water-based paint and white spirit to thin oil-based paint.

Experiment with different ratios of paint to thinners to find the one that works best. Work in small batches, carefully recording each ratio used. Test one batch before preparing the next. The only reliable way to test thinned paint is to apply it to the surface you want to cover to see if it produces the finish you want. If you are using scrap material as a test area, be sure it is primed and painted the same colour as the area you want to cover. It is also helpful to view the results of the test under the same lighting conditions as those that will affect the project. Once you have found the most suitable mix, you can prepare a larger batch of paint for the job.

**PROFESSIONAL TIP**

Before you begin, make sure that you have enough paint to complete the project. There is nothing worse than having to stop because you have run out of paint. Also, buying paint a tin at a time can make exact colour matching difficult. Different batches of the same brand and colour may vary, particularly with custom colours, because the paint dealer may not be able to make an exact match of the original shade.

## PREPARING THE PAINT

### 1 Opening the paint tin

To open a tin of paint, use a blunt, strong-edge tool, such as a 5-in-1. Gently prise up the lip of the lid in several places, until you can lift it off. Some plastic containers have a special slot into which you can insert a broad-bladed screwdriver to prise off the lid.

### 2 Stirring to blend

Stir small tins by hand with a plastic stirrer. Stir in a circular motion, occasion-ally scraping the bottom of the tin from side-to-side, until the paint has a smooth, uniform consistency and colour. Consider using a power stirrer for large containers. Non-drip paint should not be stirred.

### 3 Avoiding dirt and lumps

Before working with a previously opened tin of paint, filter out any dirt and lumps. Use a double layer of fine nylon (a pair of old tights, for example) over a bucket or paint kettle. A rubber band or some string will keep the material stretched tightly over the top of the container.

### 4 Thinning paint

Start with 1 litre (2.2 pints) of paint and add the thinners a little at a time. You can add more if necessary, but you cannot remove any excess. When testing a mixture, allow the paint on the test area to dry before assessing the results.

### MIXING PAINT

When using more than one tin of paint of the same colour, blend all the paint together by mixing or 'boxing' the cans. You will find that the colour of shop-mixed paint may vary slightly from tin to tin, and 'boxing' ensures an even colour throughout.

Pour all the paint into a large container, such as a 23 litre (5 gallon) bucket. Mix thoroughly, then pour it back into the original containers. If you do not have a large container, stir the paint in all the tins and pour a little from each tin into the paint kettle or roller tray. Stir again and use. Repeat the process when you have used up all the paint in the kettle or tray.

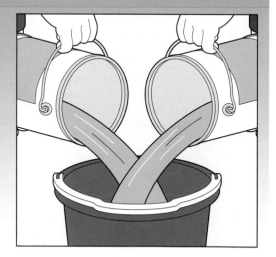

# Brush technique

The type of brush you use will be determined by the type of paint that you are applying and the surface to be painted. As a general rule, oil-based paints go on better when applied with natural-bristle brushes. Water-based paints should be applied only with synthetic brushes because water damages natural bristles (*see p.26*).

**Applying the paint** To ensure that there will be no overlap marks when the paint dries, when painting walls and ceilings with a brush, apply the paint to a small area at a time. Aim to maintain a wet edge of paint as you work. When you have applied the first brushload of paint, apply each succeeding brushload to the adjacent unpainted area and work back to the wet edge of the previous brushload. Never touch wet paint with a freshly-loaded brush.

**Painting a straight edge** In most cases, painting a straight edge means following a guide, such as the junction of a wall and a skirting board, that is already in place. Where there is no guide, use a plumb line as a guide for marking vertical lines and a spirit level for horizontal lines (*see p.39*).

## HOLDING AND LOADING BRUSHES

**Gripping a narrow brush**
Hold a narrow brush at the ferrule, between your thumb and forefinger, as if you were holding a pen. Curl your two smallest fingers up out of the way. You may need practice to do this comfortably.

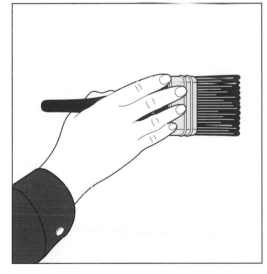

**Gripping a wide brush**
You may find a large brush more comfortable to use than a smaller one, because you can place all your fingers on the ferrule. There is no need to grip tightly. Keep your hand relaxed, maintaining just enough grip to guide the brush.

**Loading the brush**
Having transferred paint from the tin to a small paint kettle, dip the bristles into the paint up to about one-third of their depth. Tap the brush against the sides of the kettle. Do not drag the bristles over the rim, as this removes too much paint from the brush.

## APPLYING PAINT WITH A BRUSH

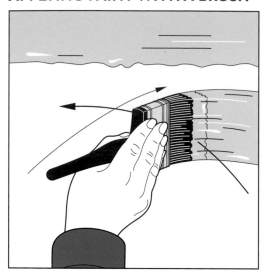

### 1 Lay paint on

Apply the paint by laying it on with a few horizontal strokes: use one side of the brush and then the other side on the return stroke. Don't worry about filling in the empty spaces yet. Your goal here is to get the paint onto the surface.

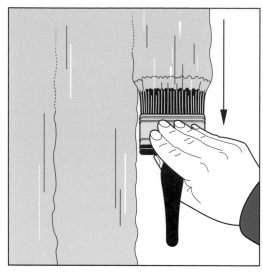

### 2 Smooth it out

Without reloading the brush, use vertical strokes to spread the paint evenly over the surface. Brush away from the wet paint you applied previously and then work back. Flex the bristles of the brush slightly to get complete and even coverage.

### 3 Feather the edge

Tip off, or feather, the edges of the painted area: lightly brush as shown above, but with only the very tips of the bristles, lifting the brush as you reach the edge of the painted area. This will blend the paint into the wet edge and create a new one.

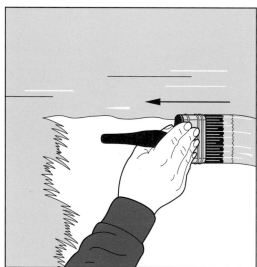

### 4 Keep a wet edge

Apply new paint to a dry area and work back towards the previously applied paint. If you are painting woodwork, brush in the direction of the wood grain. Use the same feathering technique to blend and create a wet edge.

## STAINING WOOD

Stain adds colour to the wood while allowing the grain to show through. Staining is popular on good-quality wood, such as that used in fine cabinetry, which is clean-grained, without knots or checks. Most woodwork in homes, however, is made from lesser quality wood and should be painted rather than stained.

Perfect your staining technique by practising on scrap wood of the same type. Work in small sections and experiment with different densities. One technique involves applying stain liberally, allowing it to dry for a few minutes and then wiping off with a clean cloth. Results will vary depending on the wood's porosity and the amount that is removed with the cloth.

Some woods, such as pine and other softwoods, absorb stain unevenly. Watch for this when testing. Try to compensate by wiping stain away quickly from porous areas but leaving it a little longer on less-porous sections.

**Brush with the grain**
Although you should follow the directions on the tin, stain should usually be applied by following the grain of the wood with a brush. Apply with even strokes for a uniform finish.

## HOW TO PAINT A VERTICAL STRAIGHT EDGE

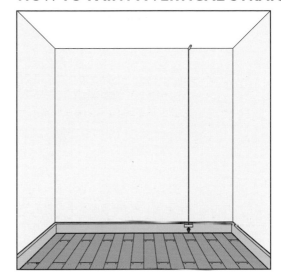

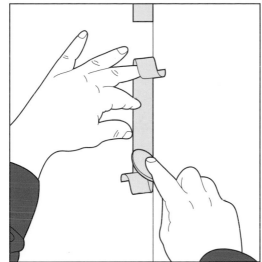

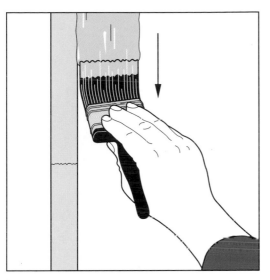

**①  Drop a plumb line**
For vertical lines, use a plumb line. Insert a nail where the top of the line will be, and attach the string to it. When the bob becomes still, the string is vertical. Hold the line steady and tape it to the wall, just above the bob.

**②  Tape in small sections**
Using the plumb line as a guide, apply masking tape to the wall. Apply the tape in short lengths, because it is easier to maintain a straight line when working with small pieces of tape. Press the tape down to ensure that it bonds well to the surface.

**③  Paint the straight edge**
Use a 75mm (3in) brush to paint the edge. Hold the brush at an angle as shown and slowly drag it down the wall about 3mm (¹⁄₈in) away from the line. Flex the bristles slightly, and the paint will bead to the line.

## HOW TO MAKE A HORIZONTAL STRAIGHT LINE

**①  Finding the horizontal**
Use a spirit level and pencil to draw horizontal lines on the wall. The tool is perfectly level when the bubble is in the centre of the horizontal vial.

**②  Extending a horizontal line**
For lines longer than the length of the spirit level, attach one end of a string to the wall and hold the other end. Use the level to adjust the position of the string until it is horizontal. Alternatively, use a line level – a small level that hangs from the string.

> **PROFESSIONAL TIP**
>
> If you don't have a plumb line, make one by tying a nail to one end of a length of string. Fasten the other end to the top of the wall and let the string hang free to get a plumb or vertical line. Never use chalk to draw lines for a painting project. Once on the surface, the chalk is impossible to remove and will ruin the painted finish.

# Roller technique

Using a roller on the walls and ceiling of a room will help you to finish the job more quickly than if you use a brush. The type of roller sleeve and the length of the pile will be determined by the type of paint to be used and the surface to be covered.

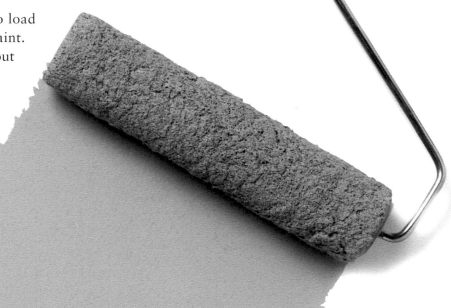

**Using a roller**  You should be careful to load the roller with the correct amount of paint. Apply the paint quickly and evenly without leaving surface marks.

**Power-rolling technique**  The keys to working with a power roller are learning to control the flow of paint and keeping the roller in motion while the paint is flowing. You should not allow the paint to flow to the roller constantly, as you may create a mess, as well as an uneven finish.

## HOLDING AND LOADING A ROLLER

**1  How to hold a roller**
Start with an open palm and place the handle across the bottom of your index finger at a slight angle away from your fingers. Then close your palm. You can rest your thumb on the top of the handle or on the side.

**2  How to load a roller from a tray**
Dip the roller into the paint and roll it slightly so that most of the roller is covered. Now slowly roll the roller back and forth on the slope of the tray to distribute the paint evenly. It should be well-loaded with paint, but not so overloaded that it drips.

**3  How to use a roller screen**
Use the same technique as for loading from a tray: fill the roller, but do not overload it. Be careful not to dip the roller too deeply into the paint, as you may have a problem with it running down the handle.

## APPLYING PAINT WITH A ROLLER

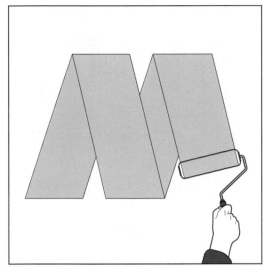

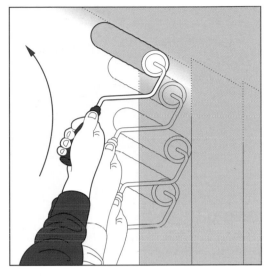

### ❶ Apply the paint
Apply the paint in sections about 1 metre (3 feet) square. Begin by laying on the paint using a zigzag motion, so that it makes a large 'M' on the wall.

### ❷ Smooth the paint
Without reloading the roller, smooth the paint by making horizontal passes with the roller. Reload the roller and paint the next area in the same way.

### ❸ Feather the edge
Using vertical strokes, lightly feather the second application into the first. Lightly roll the paint while lifting the roller slightly at the top and bottom of each painted area. This will blend the new paint with the wet edge and form a new wet edge.

## USING A POWER ROLLER

### DEALING WITH PAINT BEADS

It is not unusual to find that roller lines, which are small beads of paint, form on the surface you are painting, especially if the roller is saturated with paint. These beads may show up as roller lines when the paint dries.

Beading occurs when you apply too much pressure to the roller. This forces paint to the ends of the roller, where it forms drops. Prevent beading by applying less pressure to the roller, and by not over-loading the roller with paint. You can also try using a wider roller. The larger size seems to minimise beading. Remove beads while they are still wet by feathering the edge as explained above.

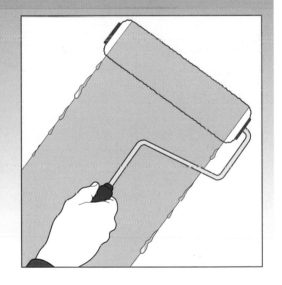

### Apply paint with a power roller
Always be sure to follow the manufacturer's directions, but in general let the paint flow to the roller head in brief spurts, avoiding a constant, heavy flow. Then use standard roller techniques to smooth the paint and blend in with what is already there.

# Power sprayers

A power sprayer will help you to cover the walls of a room quickly. But the possibility of overspray means that you must cover doors, windows and woodwork completely rather than simply applying masking tape along the edges. You must wear a respirator when using a sprayer, to avoid inhaling paint mist and solvent. Because it takes so long to prepare a room properly, using a sprayer for interiors instead of rollers and brushes does not usually save any time .

Every power spray will produce some overspray, but you can reduce this by adjusting the tip of the gun to produce the correct spray pattern, and by following the manufacturer's directions regarding air pressure and technique. Ensure adequate ventilation of the room, but don't spray if there are noticeable cross-draughts as a result of having the windows open.

**Learn the pattern**
Each tool has a different spray pattern and it is important that you become familiar with it before beginning to paint. Read the instructions to find the correct distance at which to hold the spray gun.

## SPRAYER TECHNIQUE

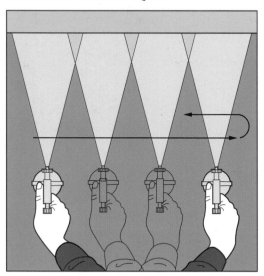

**Spray from side to side**
Spray using a side-to-side motion. As you move the gun to the right and left, bend your wrist and elbow to keep the gun tip perpendicular to the wall. Begin moving your arm before spraying and keep it moving after releasing the trigger to avoid paint buildup.

**How to paint an outside corner**
To paint an outside corner, stand directly in front of the corner and paint across it in short, side-to-side strokes. Hold the tip of the gun perpendicular to the corner, and keep it moving all the time.

**How to paint an inside corner**
Face an inside corner and move the sprayer vertically from the top of the wall to the bottom. To avoid paint buildup near the bottom of the wall, make sure that you release the trigger at the end of the pass.

# Paint pads

Paint pads are handy tools for painting woodwork and the edges of walls. The small, tapered pads are particularly useful for painting hard-to-reach sections of trim. If you are using an oil-based paint, make that the pad is suitable for use with such paint, because some harsh solvents can ruin the pad. To paint with a pad, simply dip it into the paint and pull it along the surface to be painted. Some large pads have small wheels on the side of the painting surface that guide the pad along a raised edge, such as the trim around doors and windows.

However, it is difficult, when painting large, open surfaces, such as walls or ceilings, to produce an even finish with a pad. Also, because the pads hold less paint than brushes or rollers, and do not cover surfaces so efficiently, they take more time than other painting tools to do the job. Although working back and forth with a roller or brush ensures even coverage, the same is not true of pads.

## PAINT PAD TECHNIQUE

**How to hold a large paint pad**
Hold the handle of a large pad in the same way as you would hold that of a large roller. Place the handle in your palm and close your thumb and forefinger around it. Your thumb should rest on the handle where it is most comfortable.

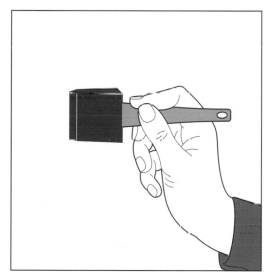

**How to hold a small paint pad**
When using a small paint pad for trim painting, hold the handle between your thumb and forefinger. This provides the most control for detail work.

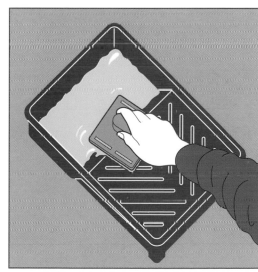

**How to load a pad with paint**
If using a large pad, dip the surface of the pad into the paint in a roller tray. Remove the excess on the raised area of the tray. For smaller pads, use a paint kettle and dip the pad an inch into the paint. Remove the excess by tapping the pad against the side.

# Solving painting problems

Many painting jobs develop problems at some stage. Even the most experienced painter makes mistakes. However, most problems can be either prevented or solved.

Some imperfections, such as blisters or specks in the paint, can be avoided by proper preparation of the surface to be painted. Other flaws, such as brush marks, runs and drips, are the result of poor application. Some problems simply occur no matter how careful you are. The solution is to watch for and deal with minor problems before they become serious. (The problems discussed below and on p.45 are all shown actual size.)

## PROBLEMS TO CORRECT BEFORE YOU BEGIN

**Blisters** Improper surface preparation causes paint to blister and peel. Applying paint to walls or woodwork that are wet, dirty or covered with numerous coats of old paint or wallpaper can result in a bubbling, peeling mess in a short time. Avoid this problem by removing as much old paint or wallpaper as possible and then cleaning the walls thoroughly.

**Specks** Even a slight breeze can stir up particles of dirt and grit that will stick to wet paint. Left-over paint that has not been strained may also contain dust and dirt that will end up on the surface you are painting. Protect your project by vacuuming the room thoroughly before you begin painting, and strain all paint from previously opened tins (*see p.36*).

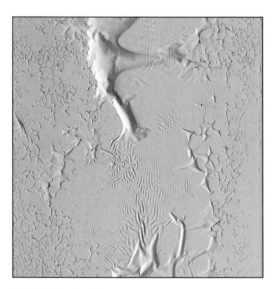

**Fix leaks first**
A wet patch on the wall prevents paint from adhering properly, which may result in a blistering surface. Sources of moisture, such as leaking roofs or defective plumbing, should be corrected before painting begins.

**Removing grit**
Before the paint dries, remove the grit with the corner of a putty knife and brush out the mark. If the paint is dry, clean the area with sandpaper and touch up with fresh paint, blending it into the surrounding area.

## SOME OTHER PROBLEMS

*Here's how to deal with other problems that can occur during a painting project:*

- It is not unusual for paint to change colour slightly as it dries. If you think you may have bought the wrong-colour paint, allow a small portion to dry thoroughly and then decide if it is the colour you wanted.
- Light can affect the appearance of a paint colour. Always examine paint samples under all the lighting conditions, both natural and artificial, that will be encountered in the area where the paint will be applied *(see p.15)*.

- Even professional painters occasionally miss a spot when painting, especially when they are covering a large area. The only recourse is to go back and touch up as necessary. Overlap marks should not be a problem on a matt or eggshell finish, but if a glossy surface shows the touch-up overlap marks, you may have to repaint the entire section of surface. It is always a good idea to keep a little extra paint on hand for this purpose.

## PROBLEMS TO AVOID DURING APPLICATION

**Brushmarks** One way to avoid leaving brush marks is to apply paint in a thin, even coat. When painting woodwork, always paint in the direction of the grain. This will help to hide brush marks. Sometimes, the brush is the problem. If you intend to use an old brush, test it first by painting a small area. If the results are not satisfactory, use a new brush.

**Runs and drips** Even the most careful professional painters must deal with drips and runs. Since drips do not become a problem until they dry, check for them every 15 minutes or so. After you have re-filled your paint kettle or roller tray, inspect the last section of surface you completed. If the paint is still wet, simply brush out the drips.

**Sanding to hide brush marks**
Sand new wood smooth to help prevent brush marks on the finished surface. Remove any sanding dust with a clean, damp cloth. Always paint in the direction of the wood grain.

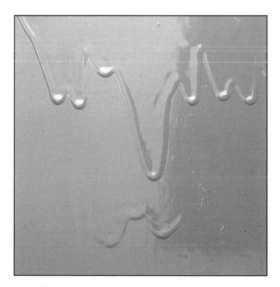

**Dealing with dry drips**
Drips or runs that have become tacky should be allowed to dry completely before you try to correct them. You can then sand out any imperfections and touch up the surface with fresh paint.

**CHAPTER 4**

# PREPARATION

Preparing a room for painting starts with creating a safe and efficient workplace. That means removing everything you can, including pictures, lights and window coverings, from the rooms in which you will be working, and protecting furniture and surfaces that you don't want to be damaged or splattered with paint. The time and effort you spend on preparation at this stage of the project will be repaid in good results.

# Preparing the room

Empty rooms are easier to paint than rooms full of furniture. If you can paint a new house or flat before moving in, by all means seize the opportunity. In most cases, however, you will need to cover or clear furniture, pictures and other objects before applying the paint.

The condition of the room to be painted will determine when to begin this phase of the project. As you will see in the next chapter, all damage to walls, woodwork and floors must be repaired before painting. Repairing plasterboard or plaster and sanding floors creates a lot of dust. Covering your furnishings before work begins will save the cost of cleaning bills later. If you are planning extensive repairs, you will want to give yourself time to do the work properly. This could mean moving and covering furniture a few days before you begin to paint.

Removing pictures and moving furniture will reveal areas that may need repair. If you are unsure of what may need to be done before painting, make a preliminary inspection behind furniture a week or or two before the project begins. Note what needs to be done in a notebook. You may want to draw diagrams of the areas that need work. The notes will be useful when you go to buy repair materials and supplies.

This is a good time to decide whether you need to employ a professional carpenter, plasterer or decorator to do some of the more complicated work. If you intend to employ professionals, follow the steps in this chapter before they arrive. They may create dust and dirt, and, possibly, not care about protecting your property as much as you do.

If the walls and the woodwork of the room require only minor repairs, you can wait until you are ready to begin painting before moving and covering the furniture. For an average-sized room, start about an hour before painting.

Start by taking down pictures and other wall decorations, then work your way towards the centre of the room. Remove books, china and other display items, even if the furniture that holds them will remain in the room. Transfer anything that can be taken out of the room to another area until the job is complete. The fewer objects left in the room the better.

Whatever is left should be moved away from the walls and covered. Deal with any ceiling fittings before you move furniture to the centre of the room, otherwise there will be no space for your ladder.

## ROOM-PREPARATION CHECKLIST

- Remove all pictures and any other wall hangings.
- Remove all switch plates and socket plates (p.50).
- Switch off the electricity, remove any wall lights, and insulate the wires (pp.50-51).
- Remove all blinds and curtains from windows.
- Protect all the ceiling lights (p.51).
- Roll up carpets and cover them with dust sheets.
- Protect exposed floors by covering them with dust sheets.
- Move all the furniture into the centre of the room and cover it with dust sheets (p.48).
- Mask woodwork if necessary (p.49).
- Make sure that the work area is well lit (p.51).
- Make sure that the room is well ventilated.

## PROTECTING FURNITURE

Any furniture that must remain in the room should be placed in the centre, and covered with either plastic or fabric dust sheets. Make sure that you cover both the top and sides of the furniture. Don't be tempted to use old sheets to cover furniture, because paint may soak through them.

Cover floors with either fabric dust sheets or old newspapers. In either case, overlap the edges and tape them together. You should avoid using plastic dust sheets on floors, because they can be slippery underfoot.

The ideal arrangement will protect your furniture while allowing you enough room to work comfortably. If you intend to paint the ceiling, you will need to be able to reach it without stretching over pieces of furniture stacked in the middle of the room. Using a roller on an extension pole will help you to avoid this problem. When painting a wall, the furniture should be far enough away to give enough space for you to work and move a stepladder easily. When moving furniture, remember that tall pieces may block the light you will need when painting. To avoid this problem, first move the furniture and then position your work lights.

### WHAT TO WEAR

Common sense dictates the kind of clothes you should wear while painting. The best choices are long-sleeved shirts or sweatshirts and long, loose trousers that you don't mind getting stained with paint. Wear a painter's hat or an old baseball cap to protect your hair. Protect yourself from noxious paint fumes and splashes of caustic liquids by wearing goggles and a respirator. Painters' gloves or rubber gloves will protect your hands. A pair of old trainers with gripping rubber soles are the safest type of shoes to wear for working on ladders and planks.

### Getting the room ready

The goal here is to protect what you don't want painted while giving yourself a clear working area. Arranging furniture in a long narrow configuration gives access to ceiling areas from either side. Keep space clear under ceiling lights because you may have to paint around them with a brush and you will need to set up a ladder to reach the area.

# Masking

Protect with masking tape any surface that adjoins one you will be painting. Be careful not to confuse masking tape with the beige parcel tape used for sealing packages. Masking tape is specially designed for decorating projects and will give the best results. The adhesive used on this tape allows the tape to be applied and removed from a surface without damaging the paint or wallpaper underneath, but it should not be left on for a long period (*see right*). Masking tape is available in several widths, to fit a wide variety of surfaces

Many people, especially professional painters, do not use masking tape because applying it is time-consuming and adds to the cost of the painting project. However, if you are a novice painter, it is best to mask before painting, to ensure a clean, crisp painted edge. For easy handling, apply the tape in small sections. If you are painting the walls and ceiling of a room, mask the adjoining woodwork, including the doors and window frame. If you are painting the woodwork, mask the adjoining walls.

Choose the width of tape that is suitable for the surfaces that need protection. Generally, for easy removal, it is best to leave loose the tape edge farthest away from the surface to be painted.

### WHEN TO REMOVE MASKING TAPE

Leave masking tape in place until the paint around it is dry to the touch. Removing the tape too soon may allow wet paint to run onto the surface you were protecting. On the other hand, you should avoid leaving masking tape on longer than is necessary, because the adhesive may damage the finish it was covering.

## USING MASKING TAPE

**Applying the tape**
Use a filling knife to smooth the tape onto the surface to be protected. Work with short lengths of tape to keep the edge as straight as possible (*p.39*).

**Masking woodwork**
Smooth the edge of the tape that is closest to the paint against the surface, but turn the outer edge up. This makes it easier to remove the tape when you have finished.

**Masking windows**
Use narrow masking tape to protect the glass in windows and doors. Apply it in short lengths. A blunt-edged tool is useful for pressing the tape into corners.

# Wall and ceiling fittings

Before starting to paint, it is best to remove wall lights (be sure to turn off the electricity first), but to leave ceiling lights in place. Wall lights can usually be removed and replaced easily. Ceiling fixtures, such as chandeliers and ceiling fans, however, may be easy to remove, but they can be heavy and cumbersome to reinstall, so it makes more sense to leave them in place and cover them.

**Covering ceiling lights**  Use plastic dust sheets or large polythene bags to cover hanging ceiling fittings (*see below*). Protect the paddles on ceiling fans in the same way.

**Removing wall lights**  Remove wall lights so that you can paint as close to the mounting box as possible. This will give a neat, well-finished appearance. Turn off the electricity at the mains before removing the fixture (*see p.54*). Protect the end of each bare wire by wrapping it in insulating tape. If you cannot remove a wall light, cover it with a plastic sheet or polythene bag.

## WHAT TO REMOVE OR COVER BEFORE PAINTING

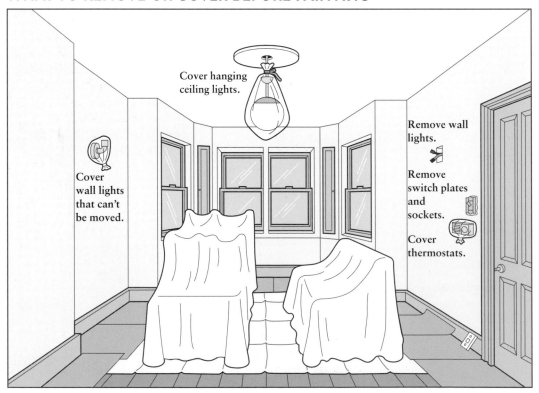

Cover hanging ceiling lights.

Cover wall lights that can't be moved.

Remove wall lights.

Remove switch plates and sockets.

Cover thermostats.

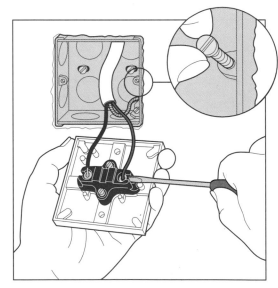

**Removing a light-switch plate**
Use a screwdriver to remove the screws and lift the switch plate away from the wall. Put the screws back in their holes *(inset)*. Then unscrew the plate from the wires *(p.54)*. Follow the same procedure when removing a socket outlet faceplate.

## DEALING WITH WALL FITTINGS

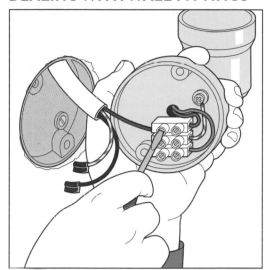

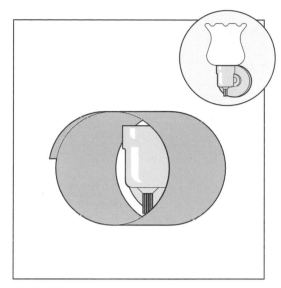

### Removing a wall fitting

Turn off the electricity at the mains. Undo the screws that hold the fitting in place, pull it away from the wall and disconnect the wires. Then insulate each exposed wire end with tape. Labelling the wires will ensure that you reconnect them correctly.

### Covering a wall fitting

If the entire wall fitting cannot be removed, just remove the shade. To protect the rest of the fitting, apply masking tape around the edge and add a protective paper tube.

## DEALING WITH CEILING FITTINGS

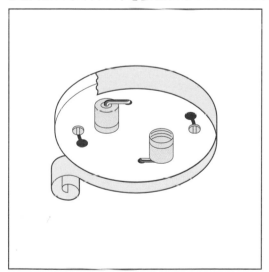

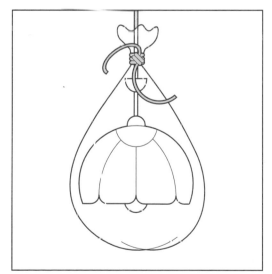

### Removing a small ceiling fitting

Remove the outer glass globes from small ceiling fittings. Remove the bulbs and apply masking tape around the edge of the fitting. After you have painted round the light, replace the bulbs and use as a light source for the room.

### Covering a ceiling fitting

Most ceiling fittings have a collar or a baseplate to cover the rough opening in the ceiling. To protect the fitting, unscrew the collar and lower it slightly. Then wrap the rest of the fitting in plastic and secure it with a piece of string.

## LIGHTING THE JOB

The room being painted needs as much light as possible. Good lighting will help you to see immediately any patches that you have missed. It will also help you to spot any drips, beading paint and other flaws while the paint is still wet enough for them to be removed. Since you will remove all curtains and blinds before you start, you will be using all of the available natural light. Add to the illumination by switching on all lights in the room and by using portable work lights. If, as a safety precaution, you have turned off all electric power to the room, use portable lights plugged into sockets in adjoining rooms.

Create as much indirect light as possible. For example, if you are painting the walls, bounce the light off the ceiling, to reduce glare and to throw a uniform amount of light on the surface being painted. If you shine light directly onto the wall, you may cast a shadow as you move about between the lamp and the wall.

# Safety when painting

Interior decorating is one of the safest home improvement projects that you can undertake, but there are still some potential hazards that must be avoided and a number of precautions that must be taken to make sure the job goes smoothly and safely.

Start by reading the label on the tin of paint that you are going to use (*see p.21*). The label not only instructs you how to use the product safely, but also provides you with first-aid advice. It is important to familiarise yourself with the procedures outlined on each tin because they may differ from product to product. Other general safety rules to follow include:

- Keep all containers tightly closed when not in use.
- Keep paints and solvents away from heat and children.
- Keep a list of emergency phone numbers on hand.

## PERSONAL PROTECTION EQUIPMENT

While the basic uniform for a painter includes long-sleeved shirts or sweatshirts, long trousers and gloves, you may require some other safety equipment. These are the most common pieces of personal protection equipment:

**Goggles** are useful when you are painting overhead. They should also be worn when you are using chemical strippers or scraping loose paint.

**Dust masks** should be worn when you are scraping away loose paint or sanding wood or paint.

**Respirators** should be used in unventilated or badly ventilated areas, or if you are sensitive to fumes from paints and solvents. When using oil-based paints and solvents, make sure that the respirator is labelled: 'Made to British Standard BSEN 149:1992'.

Respirator

Dust mask

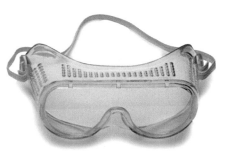

Goggles

**CHILDREN AND PETS**

It is common sense to keep paints and solvents out of the reach of children and pets. Unfortunately, painting areas seem to attract both, which can result in an overturned paint kettle, or hand or paw prints on a freshly-painted surface. More seriously, the fumes from harsh chemical strippers and solvents can injure a child's respiratory passages, and chemical stripper can burn their skin. It is essential, therefore, to keep children and pets well away from the area. Fumes can also be dangerous to a pregnant woman and her unborn child, and painting should be postponed until after the baby is born.

**EMERGENCY PROCEDURES**

If you or someone else swallows some paint or solvent, call for emergency medical help immediately. Don't panic, and don't induce vomiting unless specifically instructed to do so by a doctor. If paint gets into your eyes, rinse them out thoroughly with clean water for at least 15 minutes. If the irritation persists, call a doctor.

## LEAD IN PAINT

Until the 1960s manufacturers used lead-based pigments and also added other lead-based compounds to solvent-based paints to improve their drying time. We now know that ingesting lead in old paint by either swallowing chips of it or breathing dust from sanding it can result in any one of a number of physical and mental problems, including malfunctioning of the kidneys, hyperactivity and learning disabilities. Young children, pregnant women and the elderly are most at risk.

Lead paint is a problem only if you sand it, or if it is peeling or chipping from surfaces. Inside the house, lead paint is usually found on woodwork, doors and windows.

If your home has surfaces covered with lead paint that is in bad condition, do not remove the paint by scraping or sanding. Use a liquid paint stripper and dispose of the wet scrapings in a sealed tin. If the painted surface is in good condition, there is no need to remove it. Clean the surface and paint it with two coats of a good-quality paint. Select a product that will allow you to clean the surface in the future without damaging the paint.

It is a good idea to make sure that young children are screened for the amount of lead in their bloodstreams. Most paediatricians recommend this simple blood test as a matter of course. Ask your family doctor if you are in any doubt.

## FLAMMABLE MATERIALS

Some paints and solvents are flammable. The label will state 'Warning: Flammable' or 'Caution: Combustible Materials.' When using flammable materials, take these precautions:

- Open all doors and windows to increase ventilation.
- If you are working in a room with pilot lights, remember to extinguish them by turning off the gas. Do not relight pilot lights until the room is completely free of fumes.
- Don't smoke.
- Don't strike a match or use a naked flame anywhere near an area where flammable materials are being used or stored.
- Don't use electrical equipment which could create sparks.
- Clean up spills promptly and dispose of rags and other cleaning equipment safely. Ask your local waste disposal authority how to dispose of large volumes of solvents.
- Close tins of flammable liquids when they are not in use.
- Keep a fire extinguisher handy; use a multi-purpose dry powder type (colour-coded light blue).

### VENTILATION

Some paints and solvents give off fumes that can lead to serious illnesses if you are exposed to them for long periods of time. Even short-term exposure can cause nausea and dizziness. You can reduce your exposure to harmful fumes by following these simple rules:

- Open all the available doors and windows for ventilation while you are painting and when cleaning any equipment.
- If you are having difficulty breathing, or if your eyes begin to water, you should leave the work area immediately. Go outside and breathe deeply. If the symptoms persist, call your doctor.
- If you can't ventilate the work area properly, make sure you always wear a respirator while you are working. This will reduce the level of harmful and unpleasant fumes you are breathing while you work.

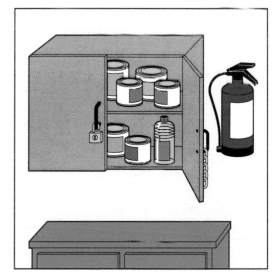

**A paint-storage cabinet**
Opened tins of paints and solvents should be stored out of the reach of children, preferably in a cabinet. The storage cabinet should have adequate ventilation and a lock on the door. If possible, mount a fire extinguisher near the cabinet.

## WORKING AROUND ELECTRICITY

When painting, you will need to remove switch plates, socket-outlet plates and, sometimes, entire light fittings. Except for when you are disconnecting wires, it is possible to complete the paint job without shutting off the electricity. However, if children or pets are around, they may be tempted to touch the uncovered outlets, which are usually near the bottom of the wall and an easy target for young fingers. In this case, it makes sense to cut off the electricity supply to the room where you will be working.

Turn off the electricity at the fuse box by either flipping the circuit breaker to the 'off' position, or removing the fuse. Standard safety procedures when working near electricity include:

- If you take a break, check that the supply is still off before resuming work.
- When shutting off the power, stand on dry planks or on a dry rubber mat. Never stand on a wet floor.
- When shutting off the power, never hold onto a metal object with your free hand. Otherwise, your body could act as a conductor for the electric current.

### TURNING OFF THE POWER

When removing wall or ceiling light fittings and switches, be sure to cut off the electricity supply to each fitting. You can do this by removing a fuse or turning off a circuit breaker in the fuse box or consumer unit, where the electric power enters your home.

To find the right fuse, turn on the lights and have a helper watch while you disconnect each fuse. Check all the lights and plug sockets; sometimes more than one circuit serves a room. If you are in any doubt about saftey, consult an electrician.

## SAFETY WITH ELECTRICITY

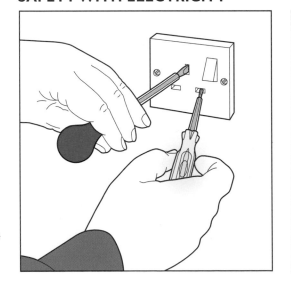

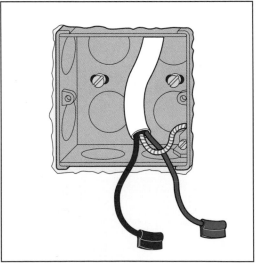

### Test before touching

Don't assume that, because the current to one outlet in a room is off, other outlets in the room are also safe. Use a voltage tester to test each outlet. If any outlet is still live, go back to the fuse box and remove the fuse that serves that outlet.

### Insulate exposed wires

After removing a ceiling or wall fitting, insulate each wire that protrudes from the ceiling or wall by covering the exposed metal ends with insulating tape.

## SAFETY WITH LADDERS AND WORK PLATFORMS

Stepladders and work platforms are among the most indispensable pieces of equipment when you are painting (*see pp.32–33*). When using them, always follow these basic safety rules:

- Never stand above the third-from-top step on a ladder. It is easy to lose your balance when standing on the upper steps.
- Never put anything but a paint kettle or roller tray on the top shelf. The shelf is not designed to take your weight.
- Don't be tempted to 'walk' or jog the ladder along a wall while you are standing on it. It is very easy to fall while trying to save the small amount of time it takes to climb down and carry the ladder to its next location.
- Don't attempt to repair a seriously defective ladder – avoid possible injury by buying a new one.
- Don't prop up a ladder on an uneven surface with an object such as a rock or a brick. Make a stable platform by standing the ladder on wide boards.
- Don't set up a ladder in front of a closed, unlocked door.
- Don't place a metal ladder near live electric wires.
- Make sure the braces on your stepladder are locked down.
- Use straight, undamaged planks for work platforms.

## SAFETY WITH LADDERS

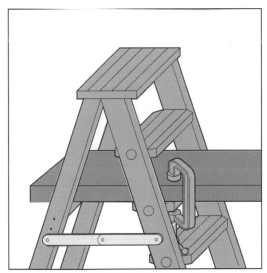

### Stepladder bracing and clamps
Clamps help to hold planks steady when you use them as work platforms. The planks should overlap the steps by at least 300mm (12in).

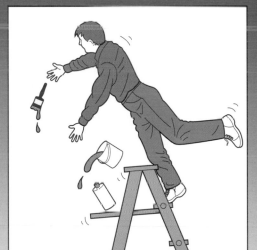

### Go no higher
Don't stand any higher than the third step from the top of a ladder, because you will not have enough support to help you keep your balance. The base of the ladder will also be unstable, and you may fall.

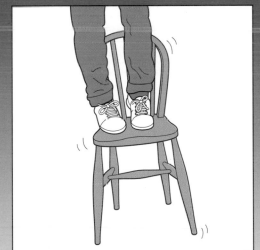

### Don't use chairs as a scaffold
Never use a chair either to reach a high place or as an anchor for a platform. Chairs are not designed for standing on.

The secret of producing a good paint finish lies in careful preparation of the surfaces to be painted. You will get the best results from your labour – and from the paint and equipment you have bought – if you carefully clean and repair any dents, cracks or holes in the surface before applying the paint. Attending to these details is just as important as the painting. Here's how to achieve perfect results.

**CHAPTER 5**

# CEILINGS AND WALLS

# First steps

Preparation is the essential ingredient of all good painting jobs. To provide a good base for the paint, ceilings and walls should be as clean and smooth as possible. You may need to take several steps to make the surface completely smooth, and it is important that you do not cut corners.

**Remove wallpaper** Avoid painting over wallpaper. If you do, you are unlikely to get a finish as perfect as you will get if you take the trouble to remove the wallpaper first. If you cannot remove the wallpaper, make sure that all of the seams lie perfectly flat against the wall.

**Prepare surfaces** Allow yourself enough time to wash down the surfaces and make necessary repairs. Stand in the centre of the room and check carefully for any damaged or greasy areas. Remove pictures and their hangers and pull furniture away from the walls to expose hidden areas. Look for dents, cracks, peeling paint and bumps. On walls and ceilings that have never been painted, look for nail holes and rough edges and seams. All of these will spoil your finished work.

**Use the correct tools and materials** Clean the ceilings and walls with a household cleaner that will remove grease and dirt. Professional painters frequently use sugar soap, a strong, concentrated water-soluble cleaner that leaves no soapy residue. Apply and rinse off the cleaner with a household sponge.

While you are washing the surfaces, examine them closely. The next few pages explain how to remove wallpaper and repair most of the damage you may find. You can use filler or joint compound for filling small holes and cracks in both plasterboard and plaster walls. Large holes in plaster walls will require plaster patches. Large holes in plasterboard should be patched with new plasterboard and sealed with joint tape and joint compound, applied with a filling knife. These knives have flat blades in a variety of widths. Use fine-grit sandpaper for smoothing out both plaster and plasterboard repairs.

In addition to the specialist painting tools listed on this page, you will also need tools found in any home tool kit, such as hammers, screwdrivers, saws and pliers.

## MATERIALS AND TOOLS

**Cleaning materials**
**Sponges**
**Dust sheets**
**Filler**
**Joint compound**
**Plaster patches**
**Joint tape**
**Filling knives**
**Sandpaper, sanding block or sponge**
**Home tool kit**
**Wallpaper stripper**
**Wallpaper steamer**
**Scrapers**
**Wire wool**
**Seam roller**
**Primer**
**Wire lath**
**Plasterboard, tape and screws**
**Brushes, rollers and roller extensions**
**Masking tape**
**Ladders**
**Paint**
**Paint solvent**

# Removing wallpaper

The type of wallpaper, the adhesive with which it was applied and what the wall underneath it is made of will determine how best to remove the wallpaper. Strippable vinyl wallcoverings that were pasted onto properly prepared walls are the easiest to remove. Simply insert the corner of a scraper under a raised seam, work a section of the paper loose, then peel it from the wall.

**Using liquid strippers** You may find that your wallpaper doesn't peel off easily or that it was hung over another, or several other layers of wallpaper. In these cases, use warm water or a liquid wallpaper stripper to dissolve the old paste, then peel off the paper. If the paper still won't come away, it is worthwhile considering hiring a wallpaper steamer.

**Using steamers** Wallpaper steamers can be hired from tool-hire companies and some DIY shops. Since hired tools rarely have complete written instructions, you may need to ask the shopkeeper to explain how to use the tool. It is more efficient if one person operates the steamer and a second follows behind to scrape off the paper.

## REMOVING WALLPAPER WITH LIQUID

**1 Score the paper**
Use a scoring tool or stripping knife to cut through the wallpaper without damaging the wall. The cuts will allow the liquid to seep through the paper and dissolve the paste.

**2 Apply the liquid**
Use a spray bottle to apply the water or stripper. Work in small areas. If the paper dries before you are able to remove it, you will have to rewet it.

**3 Remove the paper**
Use a wide-bladed stripping knife to scrape away the paper. Keep the blade of the knife flat so that the corners do not nick the surface of the wall. Clean off any paste residue with warm water.

## SEALING CRACKS IN PLASTER

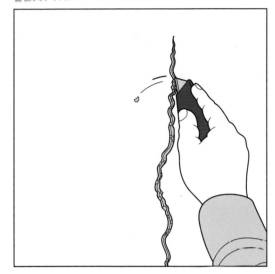

**1 Clean out the crack**
Use a Stanley knife to clean out the loose debris, then remove any fine dust with an artist's brush or a slim nozzle on a vacuum cleaner.

**2 Undercut sides of the crack**
To provide a sound surface for the filler to adhere to, hold the blade of the knife at an angle and scrape out a thin layer of sound plaster.

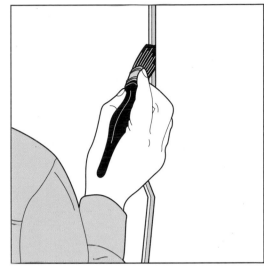

**3 Dampen with a small brush**
Dampen the undercut crack and the surrounding area with a small brush that has been dipped in water. Use the water sparingly – the surface should be damp, not wet.

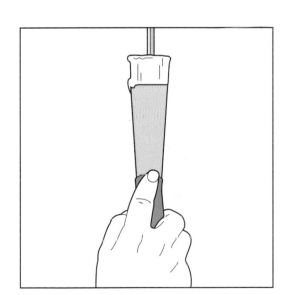

**4 Fill the crack**
Apply the filler with a filling knife, forcing it into the crack. Make one stroke down the length of the crack to remove excess filler.

**5 Sand to smooth**
Allow time for the filler to dry thoroughly, sand with a sanding block until smooth, then apply primer.

**PROFESSIONAL TIP**

**Smooth with a sponge**
You can save considerable time and effort by wiping repairs with a damp sponge before they dry completely. This will remove much of the roughness from the surface of the repair, leaving you with relatively little sanding to do.

## REPLACING PLASTER

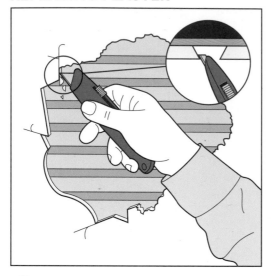

**1 Undercut the edges of the hole**
On lath-and-plaster walls, clean and undercut the edges of the damaged area and the surface of the old lath.

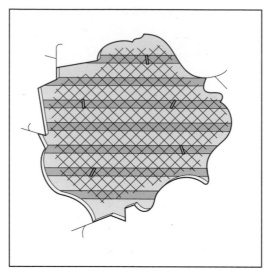

**2 Staple mesh in place**
Attach a piece of wire mesh over the wood lath, securing it with small staples as shown here.

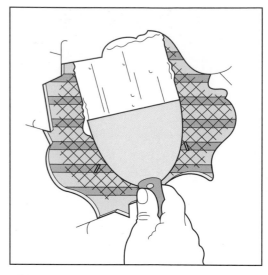

**3 Create a patch**
Mix up some patching plaster according to the directions on the packet and apply a 6mm (1/4in) thick layer to the hole. Be sure to work the patch into the undercut edge of the damaged area.

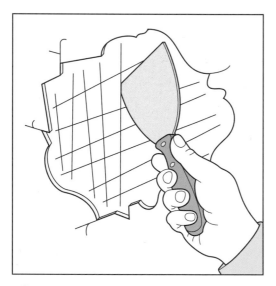

**4 Score patch with a scraper**
Score some lines into the patch with the edge of a scraper and allow it to dry. This provides a base for the next layer of plaster to adhere to.

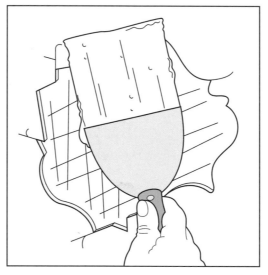

**5 Apply a second coat**
Dampen the first coat of plaster and apply a second coat. The plaster should now be roughly level with the surrounding wall. Allow to dry.

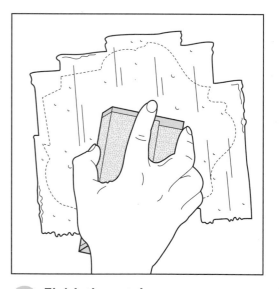

**6 Finish the patch**
Apply a finish layer of filler to the patch. When the filler has dried, use a sanding block or a sanding sponge to feather the edges of the filler with the surrounding wall to create a smooth finish. Apply primer.

# Repairing plasterboard

Plasterboard has now largely replaced plaster for ceilings and partition walls both in new buildings and renovation projects. Plasterboard is easy to install and can be repaired with patches. You will find it useful to keep a few offcuts handy for making repairs. There are many different types of plasterboard on the market. For patching, be sure to buy the same thickness as the material to be repaired. That way, the patch will lie flush with the existing wall. The following are some of the problems that may arise with plasterboard, and the solutions to them.

**Dents**  Plasterboard is easily damaged and even the most minor bump may result in a small dent. Check for depressions where the backs of chairs touch walls. Dents can be repaired with filler.

**Popped nails**  The nails used to secure plasterboard to the studs in the wall can sometimes work loose, causing the nail either to protrude or to cause a small bump on the surface. Either hammer the nail back in, or remove it before repairing.

**Large areas of damage**  If there is a large amount of damage to the plasterboard, you must add cleats to support the replaced section. Cut the plasterboard with a fine-toothed saw or a sharp knife. To trim a large sheet of board, use a straight-edge and a sharp knife to score the paper facing. Lift the panel and snap it along the scored line to break the gypsum core of the panel. Use the sharp knife to trim away the paper backing.

**Small holes**  Any hole which measures less than 125mm (5 inches) across can be repaired by using a paper flange to attach a patch.

**Damaged corners**  Outside corners formed by two plasterboards are easily damaged. They can be repaired by rebuilding the corner with tape and joint compound.

**Loose joint tape**  Sometimes, although the plasterboard is sound, the tape between the boards is peeling away. In this case, remove and replace the tape.

## TAPING A PLASTERBOARD JOINT

Plasterboard seams are concealed by a combination of joint tape and joint compound. The tape keeps the compound from cracking when it is dry. You should follow this sequence for taping a joint:

- Carefully smooth a length of joint tape over the seam.

- Using a wide-bladed filling knife, apply a thin, even layer of joint compound over the tape. Allow the compound to dry completely, then sand off any rough spots.

- Use the knife to apply a second coat of compound, this time feathering the edges. Allow this layer to dry, then sand as before.

- Apply the third coat of joint compound in the same way. Smooth the surface of the joint with a damp sponge, then allow it to dry (p.61).

### REPAIRING A DENT IN PLASTERBOARD

**1 Roughen the surface**
Before attempting to fill the dent, sand it lightly with fine sandpaper to help the joint compound to adhere.

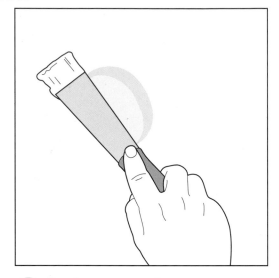

**2 Apply compound**
Apply joint compound with a filling knife. For deep dents, apply it in thin layers, allowing one layer to dry before applying the next. Once dry, sand with fine sandpaper on a sanding block and prime.

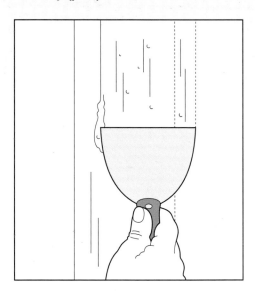

**Feather the edges**
To feather the edges on the second and third coats of joint compound, press harder on the outside edges of the knife. You may have to make two strokes to completely cover the previous coat.

### REPAIRING A POPPED NAIL

**1 Drive in the old nail**
Scrape away the paint and other material to expose the head of the nail. Drive the nail back into the wall and use a punch to tap it below the surface. Remove a nail only if you can do so without damaging the paper surface of the plasterboard.

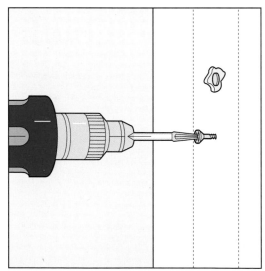

**2 Drive in a galvanised screw**
Drive a galvanised screw (they have more holding power than nails) 25-50mm (1-2in) below the loose nail. Set the screw just below the surface, without damaging the face of the plasterboard. Cover with joint compound, allow to dry, then prime.

## REPLACING DAMAGED PLASTERBOARD

### 1 Create straight edges
Since most damaged areas have irregular shapes, use a straight-edge and pencil to draw a square or rectangle around the damaged area.

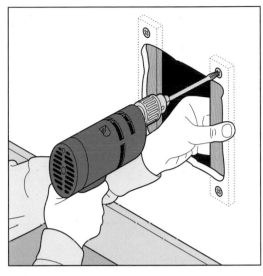

### 2 Cut a hole out of the plasterboard
Carefully drill a starter hole in each corner of the marked box. Use a fine-toothed saw, as shown, or a sharp knife to cut along the lines. Be careful not to press too hard as you may crack the plasterboard further.

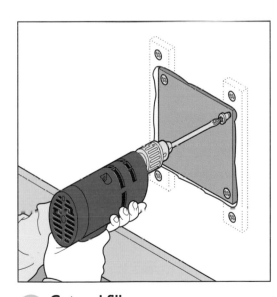

### 3 Add support
Use slim cleats to support the damaged area. Fix the cleats with galvanised screws as shown. Part of each cleat should be hidden by the wall and the other part exposed in the opening.

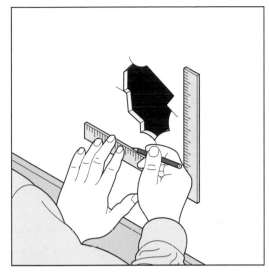

### 4 Cut and fill
Cut a patch to the exact dimensions of the hole and attach it to the cleats with screws, which should be countersunk slightly below the surface.

### 5 Apply tape
Apply joint tape to the seams. Then apply joint compound with a filling knife. Allow the compound to dry completely, then sand until smooth.

### FOR WIDER DAMAGE

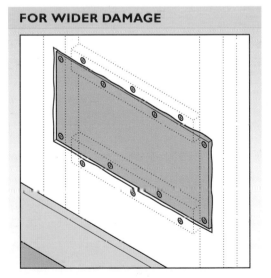

### Use studs for support
If the damaged area is extensive, cut the plasterboard back to the centre of the adjacent studs and use them for support. Screw cleats to the top and bottom edges of the hole.

## REPAIRING SMALL HOLES IN PLASTERBOARD

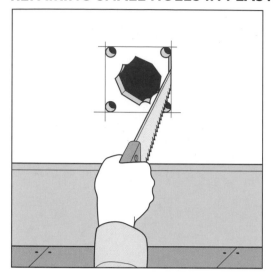

**1** **Trim the edges**
Neaten the edges of the damaged area by cutting a symmetrical hole (*p.65*). Then measure the size of the opening.

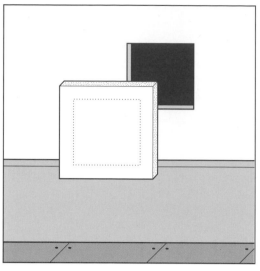

**2** **Cut a patch**
Cut a patch of board about 25mm (1in) larger all round than the opening. Place the patch on a table, white side down.

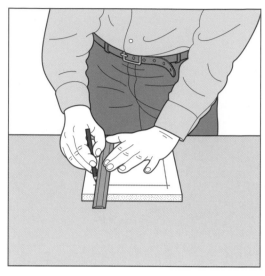

**3** **Draw the dimensions of the hole**
Draw the dimensions of the hole on the patch, centering the outline so that you leave an equal amount of excess material on all sides.

**4** **Snap the sheet**
Working on one side at a time, score the lines and snap the sheet to break the gypsum core. If you have trouble snapping the sheet, align the score along the edge of a table and press gently to break the core.

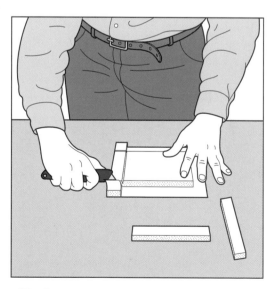

**5** **Scrape away the backing**
Scrape away the backing and the core, but leave the paper facing in place. This will create a small flange that will overlap the edges of the hole. Apply joint compound around the edges of the hole.

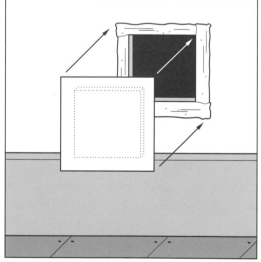

**6** **Fit the patch**
Fit the patch into the hole and press the flange onto the joint compound. Allow the compound to dry, then apply another coat. Sand the patch smooth and prime.

## REPAIRING A DAMAGED CORNER

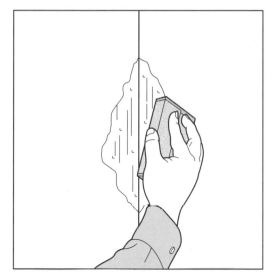

**1 Patch the corner**
Use a large trowel or a piece of wood as a guide for the joint compound. Apply compound until the damaged area is filled. Then slide the guide out of position.

**2 Sand to finish**
Wait for the compound to dry thoroughly (it usually takes 24 hours) and then sand with a fine sandpaper until the patch is level with the surrounding wall.

## REPAIRING LOOSE JOINT TAPE

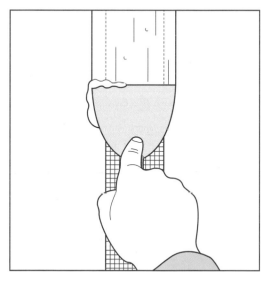

**1 Cut away any damaged tape**
Pull and cut away any loose tape from the wall. Remove all the tape until you reach a section that is still securely attached to the wall. Sand the edges of the remaining tape until the surface is smooth.

**2 Apply new tape**
Apply glass-fibre mesh tape to the plasterboard seam. Cover with a thin layer of joint compound, allow to dry, then apply further coats (p.64).

# Final preparation of walls

You should not find any popped nails on a new plasterboard wall, but you will see dozens of small depressions left by nails and screws. Those that are located along the joint between two sheets of plasterboard will be covered by joint tape and joint compound. You should fill the others with joint compound and then smooth them with a knife.

Plasterboard creates a lot of dust, which can ruin a painted finish. It is important, therefore, to clean the walls and all horizontal surfaces, including the ceiling and floor, the mantelpiece, window ledge and mouldings.

Make a final check of the room to ensure that all plasterboard joints are smooth and that they are level with the surface of the wall before you begin to paint. If you find that any joint compound has hardened on the floor or on a part of the wall where it should not be, scrape and sand it off.

Always prime bare plaster or plasterboard *(see p.24)*. After you have cleared away all preparation materials, you are ready to paint.

## PREPARING UNPAINTED SURFACES

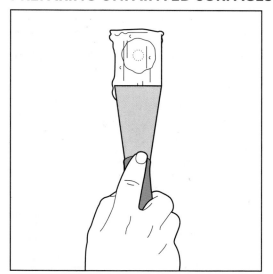

**1 Apply joint compound**
Use a filling knife to apply filler to the small dimple left by a plasterboard nail or screw.

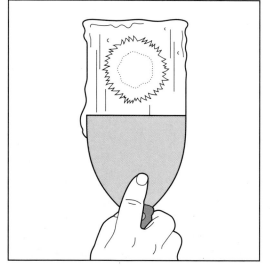

**2 Apply more coats**
Allow to dry and follow with a second and third coat, using a wider-bladed knife. Sand down rough spots and smooth with a damp sponge.

**PEELING PAINT**

Paint usually peels away from walls and ceilings because the surface was not prepared properly, a leak has loosened the paint, the wrong type of paint was used or the wall was damaged in some way. Whatever the cause, you must remove all the loose paint and prepare the wall underneath so that it will provide a sound surface for the new paint to adhere to.

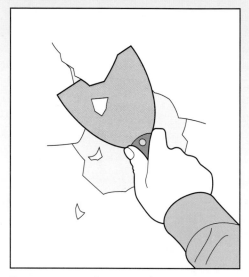

**Scrape away loose paint**
Use a flat-bladed paint scraper to remove any loose paint from ceilings and walls. When you come to a section that cannot be removed with the scraper, use a medium-grit sandpaper to smooth the edges of the paint round the scraped area. The object is to create a smooth, seamless transition between the existing paint and the bare wall. Finish with fine-grit sandpaper, then prime the bare area.

# Painting ceilings and walls

Once you have prepared the ceiling and walls, protected what needs to be kept safe from splattered paint and have all of your equipment and tools at hand, it is time to get started.

**Getting ready** Begin by setting up a work centre, an area in the room where you can mix paint, refill roller trays and keep any equipment you are not using at the moment but may need to use later. An out-of-the-way corner equipped with a sturdy table covered with a dust sheet would be ideal. Store paint that you do not need at the moment under the table, with any extra brushes, roller sleeves and rags.

## PAINTING CEILINGS

When painting an entire room, always work on the ceiling first, then, if any paint splatters on walls and woodwork, it can be cleaned up easily or painted over later.

To avoid overlap marks, start work at the narrow end of the room, moving across the width of the ceiling. If you will be painting the walls later, save time by allowing an inch or so of the paint to overlap onto the wall when cutting in. You will find it easier to paint a straight edge on the wall rather than on the ceiling. If you will not be painting the wall, use a brush to cut in at the corner where the ceiling and the wall meet. Some rooms have decorative coving at the tops of the walls. This serves as a useful guide when you are painting and makes it easy to cut in.

If two painters are working at the same time, start at opposite ends of the narrow part of the room and work towards each other. This means that your wet paint edge will be advancing towards your partner's. Don't be tempted to have one person cut in while the other rolls. The person using the brush could get ahead of the one using the roller, and the border could dry before the rest of the ceiling is painted, resulting in lap marks.

Wear a hat and goggles when you are painting a ceiling. A roller extension will help the work move along quickly, because you won't need to keep moving a ladder. Make sure that any ceiling fittings are protected by plastic dust sheets.

**Lighting ceilings** When painting the ceiling, start near a window and work backwards. Because the natural light source will be in front of you as you work, you will be able to see and correct mistakes as they happen.

**KEEPING PAINT MIXED**

Modern paints should stay mixed for several days once you have stirred or shaken them properly. But, to be on the safe side, always stir the paint before refilling your paint kettle or roller tray. Often, it does not become apparent that the paint was not mixed properly until it has dried on the wall.

**PROFESSIONAL TIP**

**Practise using an extension**
Before loading the roller with paint, practise handling the extension. Start with your hands 450mm (18in) apart and then experiment with different grips until you find one that is comfortable.

## HOW TO PAINT A CEILING

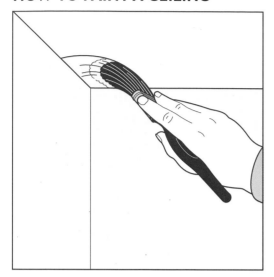

**1** **Cut in with a small brush**
Begin in the corner and use a 50mm (2in) brush to paint the border, about 150mm (6in) wide, close to the wall. Flex the bristles of the brush to draw a straight line along the edge. Accuracy is more important than speed at this point.

**2** **Paint the corners**
Go back to the corner and spread the paint out with the brush along the other side of the angle. This will help to prevent paint build-up in the corner, which may eventually drip down the wall.

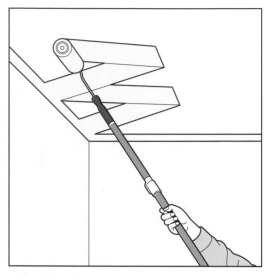

**3** **Use the roller**
Work on one small section of the ceiling at a time. Dip the roller into the paint reservoir and roll it along the sloping surface of the roller tray. The roller sleeve should be saturated with paint, but not dripping. Apply the paint in a zig-zag pattern, so that you form large 'Ms' or 'Ws'.

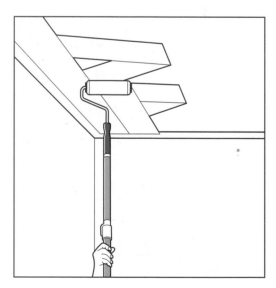

**4** **Smooth out the paint**
Without reloading the roller, make strokes across the zig-zag pattern, to smooth out the paint over the entire section.

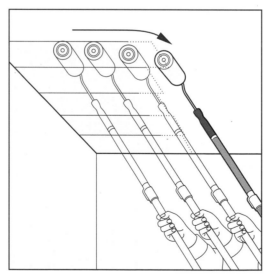

**5** **Feather the edge**
Rolling towards the unpainted areas of the ceiling, feather the edges of the painted area by lifting the roller slightly near the edge of the section. Then begin another section, working across the narrowest part of the ceiling.

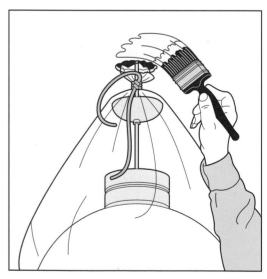

**6** **Paint round ceiling fixtures**
You will have to use a brush to paint round ceiling fixtures. A roller is suitable only for large areas where it can be manoeuvred without obstruction.

## PAINTING WALLS

When you are painting a room, the walls are the largest area to be covered. Even in a medium-size room, painting the walls is a big job. Fortunately, however, there are only a few basic techniques that you need to master in order to achieve results worthy of a professional.

You can use a roller, a brush or a spray to apply paint to a wall. If you use a roller – as most people do – you will still need to use a brush to apply the paint round the edges. If the wall is made of unpainted plasterboard or plaster, apply a primer first.

**Preparing to paint**  By now, you will have painted the ceiling and prepared the walls. You will also have masked the edges of the doors and windows and removed or masked all sockets and light fittings.

**Taking cues from the room**  Remember that the shape and layout of the room are good guides to where you should start painting. Begin on the wall with the most uninterrupted space. Save the wall that requires the most cutting in round windows and doors until last. If, however, you start late in the day, paint the smallest wall first. That way, when you stop for the day, you will still have been able to complete an entire wall.

**Where to begin**  If you are right-handed, begin in the upper right-hand corner. Left-handed painters should begin in the upper left-hand corner. This ensures that your body and your free hand are always in front of an area of unpainted wall. If you should happen to lean against or touch the wall, you will not be touching wet paint.

**Painting high walls**  The easiest way to paint a high wall is with a roller extension (*see p.69*). If you do not have an extension, stand on a sturdy stepladder to reach the top of the wall – never stand on a chair or stool.

---

**PROFESSIONAL TIPS**

- If you are planning to sell your house, give the walls a fresh coat of paint to make the house more attractive to prospective buyers. Most estate agents recommend painting in neutral colours, such as white or beige.
- If you are planning on finishing off tomorrow what you can't get done today, don't bother to clean your roller. Store it in a plastic bag overnight (*p.127*). The next day, before you resume painting, make a few practice strokes on scrap material to 'recondition' the roller sleeve.
- The techniques outlined on the following pages will help novice painters to paint walls successfully. However, some professional painters prefer to use roller extensions when they paint walls because they find that using an extension is easier on the shoulders than using a short-handled roller. When you have mastered the basic techniques, you may like to try painting walls using an extension.

## HOW TO PAINT A WALL

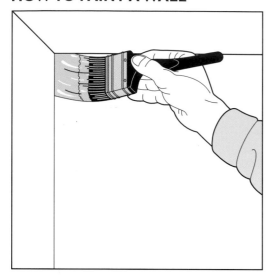

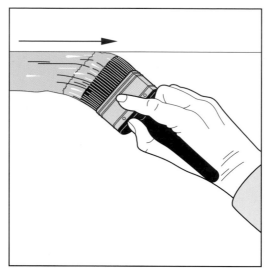

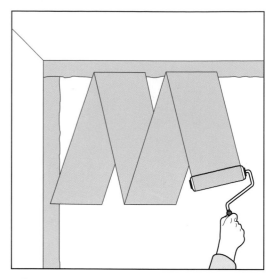

**1  Cut in with a small brush**
Using a 50mm (2in) brush, apply paint where the ceiling and wall meet, to create a wet edge, approximately 1 metre (3 feet) across and 150mm (6in) deep.

**2  Brush below the junction**
Keep the bristles of the brush just below the junction of the wall and ceiling and, using long, even strokes, apply light pressure to bend the tips of the bristles slightly. This will force the paint to bead and fill the gap between the top of the brush and the ceiling.

**3  Apply the paint with a roller**
Without waiting for this strip to dry, use a roller to paint the wall immediately below. Starting about 1metre (3feet) below the wet edge, lay on the paint in a vertical zig-zag pattern that looks like a big 'M' and covers an area approximately 1m² (3ft²).

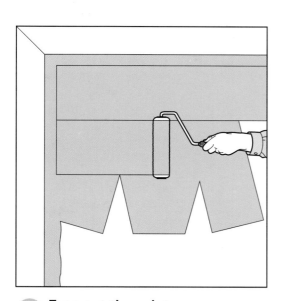

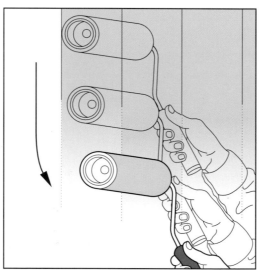

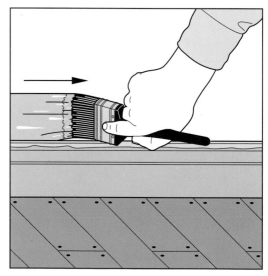

**4  Even out the paint**
Without loading the roller with more paint, smooth out the paint using horizontal strokes. Make sure that the entire section is covered and that the new paint blends with the wet edge. Work quickly, but don't rush.

**5  Feather the edges**
Use the feathering technique (p.41) along the unpainted part of the wall so that it will blend with the fresh paint. Then reload the roller and begin again, making sure that you blend in the new paint with the adjacent wet edge.

**6  Paint along the skirting board**
At the bottom of the wall, where the skirting board will obstruct the roller, use a 50mm (2in) brush to paint a border.

**7** **Paint round windows or doors**
When you reach a window or door, use the brush to paint a border close to the frame on the wall you are painting.

**8** **Fill in with a roller**
Still using the brush, paint a border close to the frame on the wall above the door and at the junction between the ceiling and the wall. Paint the area in between with the roller. Treat windows in the same way.

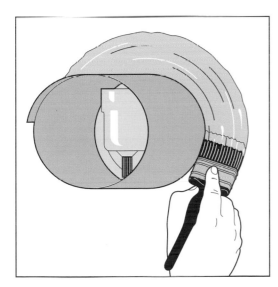

**9** **Paint around light fittings**
If you haven't already shut off the electricity supply at the junction box, do so now. Mask light fittings and disconnect, insulate and label any exposed wires (pp.50–51). Use a narrow brush to paint a border round the fittings.

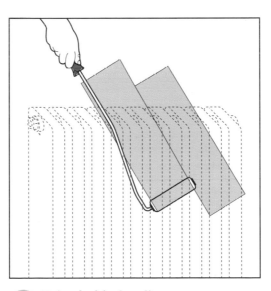

**10** **Paint behind radiators**
Apply paint with a radiator brush, or a mini-roller (p.28).

## OTHER CHOICES

**Painting walls with a brush**
Many people believe they get better results using a brush, rather than a roller, on walls. Although brushes are easier to direct and are less likely to splatter paint, the job will take longer to complete with a brush (pp.26–27).

**Power rollers and power sprays**
Although ordinary rollers and brushes are the most popular means of applying paint to walls, power rollers and power sprays will cover large areas more quickly (pp.29–30).

**Always wear goggles and a face mask when using a power spray, and remember that the paint fumes may be highly flammable.**

## PACING YOURSELF

The best time to take a break is when you have completed an entire wall. If this isn't possible, stop when you reach a window or door. Never stop painting for any length of time in the middle of a wall. If you do, the demarcation line between the two areas will show plainly when the paint dries.

# Textured finishes

Textured paints contain additives that cause the paint to dry to a rough finish, much like stucco. They can add depth or texture to what, ordinarily, would be a smooth surface. They can also be used to hide cracks and other imperfections in walls and ceilings. You can create unusual patterns in the textured surface, using ordinary household tools, or painting tools. Experiment with sponges, scrunched-up pieces of paper, or trowels. Textured paints are available ready-mixed, which are the easiest to use, and in powdered form.

**REPAINTING TEXTURED FINISHES**

If you are painting over a textured finish, use a long-nap roller, but keep a brush handy. If the texture is very pronounced, the paint may begin to drip as you apply it. If this happens, smooth it with a brush immediately after rolling.

## TEXTURED FINISHES

**Adding texture with a brush**
Roll the paint onto the ceiling or wall, then use an old paintbrush to add texture. Dab the surface with the bristles, or slap the flat side of the bristles against it.

**Using a whisk broom**
Roll the paint onto the ceiling or wall. Hold the bristles of a whisk broom at an angle of about 60° to the surface. Make one continuous sweep to form a half-circle pattern, then lift the bristles from the surface. Repeat the process, overlapping about half of the preceding half circle.

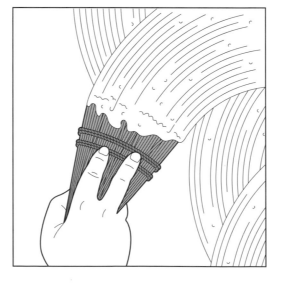

# Decorative finishes

Most of this book deals with painting the inside of your home with solid colours of paint. But you can create unusual effects by mixing ordinary paints with transparent glazes. A topcoat of glaze allows parts of a solid base coat to show through, which creates an illusion of depth, and an interesting merging of colours and shades. Both oil-based and water-based glazes are available. Use a water-based glaze with water-based paint.

Shown here are only a few of the decorative finishes you can create. Some mimic the appearance of natural materials, such as marble and wood, while others create unusual effects. No matter which you try, be sure to practise on scrap material first so that you can see how the finish will turn out.

## DRAGGING

This finish is best on doors and woodwork rather than on large expanses of wall. Prepare the surface and apply an eggshell base coat with a brush. Mix the glaze and the paint. Experiment with a glaze darker than the base coat. Keep the brush clean between strokes by wiping off excess paint on a scrap of paper or cloth.

## THE METHOD FOR DRAGGING

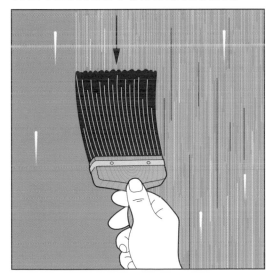

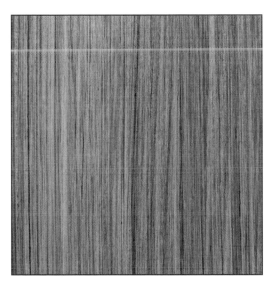

**MATERIALS AND TOOLS FOR DRAGGING**

**Paints**
**Glazes**
**Brushes**
**Varnishes**

**Drag in straight lines**
Apply the glaze. While the glaze is still wet, draw a dry dragging brush over the surface, keeping the lines as straight as possible. Once you start dragging a section, don't stop until you reach the edge. Overlap the rows of lines slightly.

**The finished effect of dragging**
When the glaze is dry, protect the surface with two coats of clear polyurethane varnish.

## SPONGING

Prepare the walls or woodwork as you would for painting, including priming. Decide on a colour scheme that includes a base coat, which will be the foundation of the treatment, and one or two other colours. These other colours can be lighter shades of the base coat, or they can contrast with it. Use a paint with an eggshell or satin finish for the base coat. When you mix the glaze into the sponging paint, add a little at a time until you get the shade you want. Test the effect on scrap material.

Work in an inconspicuous corner of the room until you gain confidence in your technique. Work slowly, and make sure you do not oversponge. This will make the impressions too dense and will create an overall muddled appearance. Wait for the first sponge coat to dry before applying the second colour.

**Take off a little paint**
For a slightly softer look, try dabbing an area with paint and then, with a sponge dipped in white spirit if you are using oil-based paint, or water if it is water-based, and squeezed until it is just damp, dab lightly over the wet paint.

### MATERIALS FOR SPONGING

| | |
|---|---|
| **Paints** | **Paint trays** |
| **Glazes** | **Varnishes** |
| **Natural sponges** | |

## THE METHOD FOR SPONGING

**1 Sponge on the first colour**
Wearing rubber gloves, dip a section of the sponge into the glaze-and-paint mixture. Squeeze it out and blot it on newspaper to remove excess paint.

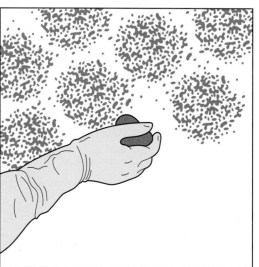

**2 Dab on the surface**
Dab the sponge on the surface to be painted, leaving small spaces between the dabs. Vary the angle of your wrist and the sponge as you work.

**3 The finished effect of sponging**
One coat of sponging will create the effect shown here. You can add a second coat in another colour once the first is dry. Finish with two coats of varnish.

## RAGGING

Prepare the surface as you would for painting and apply an eggshell base coat. Then mix the glaze with paint and apply it to the wall when the base coat is dry. Interesting effects can be obtained by using a darker or lighter version of the base coat for the glaze. For a softer effect, one person can roll on the glaze, while a second follows and lifts off part of the glaze with a rag.

Use any lint-free material for the rag. Cotton is the traditional material used for ragging, although a variety of other materials can be used. Do not use synthetic fabrics, however, since they do not absorb paint as readily as natural ones. Whatever material you choose, make sure you have plenty on hand. As you work, the rags will quickly become saturated with paint and will need to be replaced frequently.

| MATERIALS AND TOOLS FOR RAGGING | |
| --- | --- |
| **Paints** | **Solvent** |
| **Glazes** | **Varnishes** |
| **Lint-free rags** | |

## RAG ROLLING

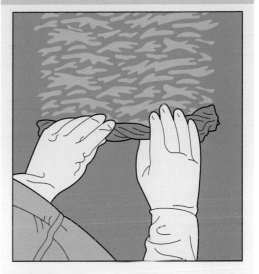

**Roll the rag up and down**
Rather than holding the rag in the palm of your hand, try rolling it into a sausage shape, and rolling it up and down the surface. Overlap the rows slightly. This will keep a wet edge and avoid lap marks. Change rags often to maintain the pattern.

## THE METHOD FOR RAGGING

**1 Dab the surface with a rag**
Crumple up a rag dampened with solvent, add paint and dab at the surface. Vary the position of your hand to make interesting patterns. Develop a rhythm with your partner. Clean or change the rag when it becomes saturated with paint.

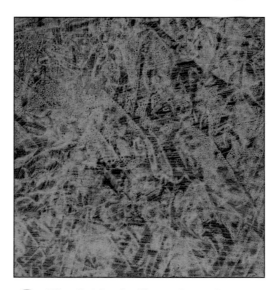

**2 The finished effect of ragging**
Protect the finish with two coats of clear polyurethane varnish if desired.

**The finished effect of rag rolling**
Rag rolling produces a consistent pattern over a large area. To maintain the pattern, use the same type of material throughout. If you are using rags from old clothing, remove seams, buttons etc.

**CHAPTER 6**

# WOODWORK, DOORS AND WINDOWS

Painting the woodwork in a room opens up a number of design possibilities. You can choose a colour that contrasts with the colour of the walls and ceiling, or one that highlights them. If the woodwork is the most distinctive feature in the room, this is your opportunity to enhance its beauty. If, on the other hand, it is quite ordinary, you can make it blend into the background. Either way, the woodwork is an integral part of your room's colour scheme.

# Paints for woodwork

While many types of wood used in furniture making are so beautiful that their grain and natural colour are left exposed, much of the woodwork found in homes has to rely on a painted finish for its beauty. This is especially true of most houses built within the last 40 years. However, older houses, and even some new ones in some parts of the country, have stained woodwork. If you are adding new mouldings or doors to this type of house, you will want to stain the new wood to match what is already there.

**Making repairs** Mouldings and architraves round windows and doors hide joints and rough openings in plaster and plaster-board, and create a finished appearance. They also protect walls from bumps and dirty hands. For this reason high-gloss paints are usually chosen for these surfaces. In fact, woodwork may be the last bastion of oil-based paint. Of course, there is a number of very good reasons for selecting water-based paints, including ease of cleaning up. Consider the differences between the two types of paint (*see p.22*) before choosing.

**Painting technique** Painting the woodwork in a room requires a different technique to that used for covering walls and ceilings. On small surfaces, the sweeping motion of a roller must give way to the precision of a brush.

## THE ORDER FOR PAINTING WOODWORK

When painting woodwork, start at the top of the room and work down: wooden cornices, picture rails, doors, windows, dado rails, then skirting boards. To save wear and tear on your knees when painting skirting boards, wear knee pads or kneel on a cushion.

The edges of woodwork are sometimes curved or very narrow – less than 12.5mm (½in) – making it difficult to paint them neatly. Vertical edges of window and door frames are not only narrow, they are often also at an angle that is difficult to reach easily with a paint brush. Sometimes, it may be better to paint the woodwork before painting the walls, then you can overlap the walls slightly with the paint. You'll find it easier to paint a straight edge along a wall than along the edges of narrow or curved woodwork. Always protect freshly-painted woodwork when painting adjacent walls with a roller.

# Preparing woodwork

Whether or not it has been painted before, wood must be properly prepared before being painted. In general, this means filling any cracks and holes and then sanding the surface. Even previously painted surfaces must be sanded, especially if they were painted with a glossy paint. Sanding provides a key for the new paint to adhere to. This is very important if the original paint is oil-based and you plan to cover it with a water-based paint. As an alternative to sanding, you can apply chemical cleaner. These are liquids that help the new paint to bond to the old one.

Make sure that the surfaces are clean. Remove fingerprints and stains with a household cleaner and allow to dry. Clean greasy woodwork with sugar soap, following the directions on the label.

Just as you surveyed your walls and ceilings to judge the extent of necessary repairs, do the same with the woodwork. Pay special attention to door frames and to skirting boards near furniture, as these are subjected to a lot of wear and tear.

**Making repairs**  Fill holes or scratches in woodwork with wood filler. Some professional painters use putty to fill small holes, because it does not shrink and is easy to apply. Use mastic to fill cracks that open up between two pieces of moulding.

**Removing peeling paint**  Peeling or loose paint can ruin a new finish. Carefully scrape away loose material and sand the edges to provide a smooth transition between the sanded area and the sound paint. In some cases, you may need to strip away the old paint completely to provide a good surface for the new paint.

**Preparing windows and doors**  Window frames and doors should be clean and free of defects. Remove all hardware, such as locks and doorknobs, before you begin to paint.

## YOU WILL NEED:

*For preparatory work*

**MATERIALS AND TOOLS**
**Sandpaper**
**Chemical cleaner**
**Cleaning solutions**
**Wood filler or putty**
**Decorators' mastic and
    mastic gun**
**Electric palm sander**
**Vacuum cleaner or rags**
**Putty knives**
**Paint scraper**
**Primer**
**Heat gun (optional)**
**Power sander (optional)**
**Paint stripper (optional)**
**Wire wool**

*For painting*

**MATERIALS AND TOOLS**
**Paints and stains**
**Brushes**
**Masking tape or thick paper**
**Screwdriver**
**Hammer and nails**
**Sharp knife**
**Trestles**

### MAKE THE SANDING SHEET FIT THE SURFACE

You can bend and shape sandpaper to make it easier to use. For example, to sand concave surfaces, wrap the paper round a section of hose or pipe. Large flat surfaces can be sanded with the paper wrapped round a wood block.

## PREPARING PAINTED WOOD

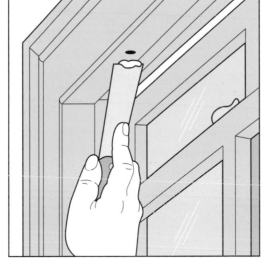

### SAFETY TIPS

- If you suspect that there are traces of lead paint on any surface, avoid scraping or sanding it (*p.53*). The dust produced by sanding can carry the lead through the house, posing a serious threat to health if it is inhaled.
- Read and follow carefully all instructions for the products which you plan to use.

**1 Roughen the surface**
Prepare glossy sheens to receive the new paint by sanding with damp wet-and dry abrasive paper. On wide sections of moulding or architraves, use an electric palm sander. Wipe the surface with a cloth or vacuum it, then repair and fill any holes and scratches.

**2 Fill any holes**
Use a putty knife to apply wood filler or putty. Smooth with the knife so that the repair is level with the surface of the wood. If the first layer of filler shrinks, apply a second layer. Allow the repair to dry completely, then apply primer.

### HIDING WOOD KNOTS

**3 Deal with loose paint**
Scrape away loose lead-free paint with a paint scraper. To avoid gouging the underlying wood surface, hold the blade nearly parallel to the surface. Remove all the loose paint, stopping only when you reach an area where the surface is sound.

**4 Sand the edges**
Finish the repair by sanding the edges of the old paint to create a smooth transition between the bare wood and the old paint. Prime the bare wood.

If wood knots have bled through the old paint finish, treat them with knotting (*p.24*). If you skip this step, the knots will eventually bleed through the new paint finish.

## STRIPPING WOODWORK

It is not usually necessary to strip sound paint from the wood-work in a room, unless you wish to reveal antique mouldings or cornices. If the old paint is in good condition, proceed as shown on pages 80–81. If the old paint finish is flaking, peeling or blistering, correct the problem by stripping it from the damaged areas.

There are three ways to remove paint: you can either use a heat gun, sand the surface, or apply a chemical paint remover. All three methods have their advantages and disadvantages. A heat gun does the job quickly, but, if not used properly, it can scorch the wood or cause a fire. A power sander is useful for removing paint from large, flat areas of woodwork. Sanding produces a smooth finish but creates a lot of dust. Chemical strippers are available as liquids, pastes and gels. Although they provide quick results, they are caustic, and some produce noxious fumes. If you do use a chemical stripper, choose a paste or gel for vertical surfaces.

When using a chemical stripper or sanding, seal the room off from the rest of the house by hanging sheets of polyethylene or plastic over doorways. This will help to prevent fumes and dust from escaping into the rest of the house, but make sure that the room is well ventilated, by opening the windows.

## USING A HEAT GUN

**Strip paint with a heat gun**
Heat guns cause the paint to bubble and blister. When it begins to bubble, remove it with a flat-bladed knife. Keep the gun moving in front of the knife. Scrape the paint from the knife into a metal container, and always switch off the gun while doing so.

## USING A POWER SANDER

**Strip paint with a power sander**
First use a coarse abrasive paper in the sander. Keep the sander moving to avoid damaging the wood surface. Sand in the direction of the grain. When all the paint has been removed, smooth the surface with fine-grit sandpaper.

## USING CHEMICAL STRIPPERS

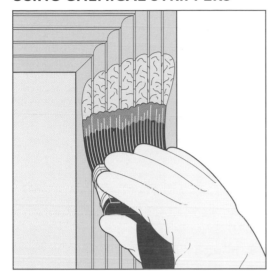

**1   Apply the stripper with a brush**
Wearing protective gloves, apply the chemical stripper with a brush and leave it for the time specified on the label, to allow it to dissolve the paint.

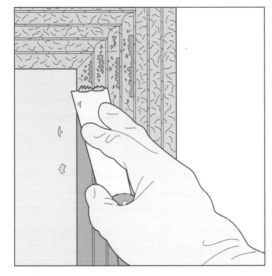

**2   Remove the paint with a knife**
Remove the loosened paint with a flat-bladed knife, and dispose of the waste in a metal container. Work carefully to avoid damaging the wood. Apply a second coat of stripper, if necessary.

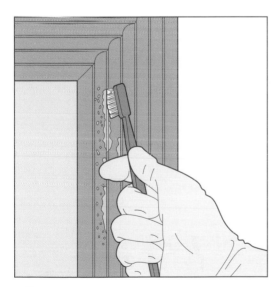

**3   Remove the paint from grooves and crevices**
Use an old toothbrush to remove paint from grooves and crevices. Do not use a wire brush, because it will scratch the wood.

**4   Wipe and wash the surface**
You may have to wipe the surface down with more stripper and wire wool before wiping it with solvent to remove all traces of the stripper. Follow the directions on the product's label. Sand the surface lightly before priming.

### STRIPPING KNIVES

If you are worried that you might damage the wood with a steel blade when you are removing paint that has been treated with a chemical stripper, try using a plastic stripping knife. Alternatively, you can use a special pad made from synthetic material. The pad will not damage the wood, it will not rust if you use it with water-based stripper, and it will last longer than wire wool.

### SAFETY TIPS

- Wear safety glasses for all stripping methods.
- Wear protective gloves when scraping away paint removed with a heat gun.
- Keep a fire extinguisher handy when working with a heat gun.
- Wear a dust mask when sanding.
- When using a chemical stripper, keep the area well ventilated and wear a respirator. Never smoke or allow others to smoke while you are working with chemical strippers.
- Wear rubber gloves and a long-sleeved shirt when using chemical strippers.
- Keep children and pets away from all stripping tools and materials.
- Dispose of stripped paint with care.

### PREPARING BARE WOOD

As with any surface, bare wood must be clean, dry and smooth before it is painted. Clean it with a household cleaner if necessary. For stubborn grease marks and oil-based spots, rub with a cloth dampened with white spirit (wear rubber gloves).

Carefully check all the mouldings and architraves. Spot sand rough edges and fill nail holes, cracks and dents (*see p.81*). Make sure that all nails are punched below the surface of the wood.

After sanding, make sure you remove all sanding dust before it becomes trapped under a coat of primer, by wiping the woodwork with a damp cloth or vacuuming it thoroughly. Professional furniture restorers use a tack cloth specially designed to remove dust. If you are painting only a window or two, or a short section of new moulding, invest in a tack cloth. For larger jobs, use a damp – not wet – cloth or sponge to remove dust.

**Filling joints** The joint where two pieces of door or window architrave meet at a corner sometimes separates. Use mastic to fill open joints. There are many different types of mastic on the market. For filling cracks in wood, choose either plain or acrylic mastic. Both are compatible with wood, and can be painted.

**Filling openings**
Fill a separated joint in a window architrave with mastic. Apply it with a gun. The mastic will seal out both air and water. After you have filled the opening, wipe the surface smooth, allow to dry, then apply primer.

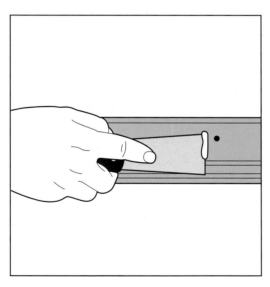

**Filling nail holes**
Fill nail holes in new mouldings and architraves with wood filler or putty. Push in a small amount with the edge of a putty knife, or your finger. You can use the same technique for small nicks and dents in the wood. Sand when dry, if necessary.

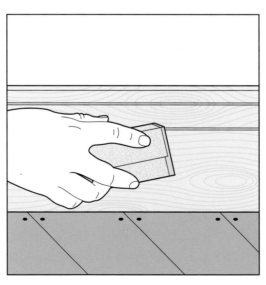

**Smoothing rough spots**
Use a fine-grit sandpaper to smooth the rough spots. Before priming, wipe the surfaces with a tack cloth or a damp rag. Allow to dry, then prime.

**Sanding difficult areas of wood**
Smooth narrow areas, such as glazing bars, by cutting the sandpaper into strips and grasping the bar between your thumb and forefinger. Sand in an up-and-down direction (or from side to side on horizontal bars). Wipe with a cloth before priming.

# Priming and painting woodwork

**The right tools**  Although the walls and ceilings of a room may be a larger area, you need just as much precision when painting the woodwork. For mouldings and architraves, you'll be using a 50mm (2 inch) brush and spending a lot of time painting straight edges along walls and ceilings. Rather than applying masking tape to these areas, use a straight-edge to mask as you go.

**Priming the surface**  Apply a coat of primer to all bare wood before painting. The primer will seal the surface of the wood, preventing the paint from soaking in, and will provide a good base for the finish coats.

If a water-based primer has raised the grain of the wood slightly, sand with a fine-grit sandpaper and remove sanding dust with a damp rag before applying the paint. Oil-based primer can be used, even under a water-based paint. However, oil-based primers usually cannot be painted over for 24 hours after they are applied (*see p.24*). Mask any adjacent surfaces that will not be painted.

**New mouldings**  It is usually easier to prime new mouldings before they are installed. Stand the section of moulding on end, or place it on a work surface covered with newspaper, then prime. Since there is no need to paint a straight edge, the primer will go on quickly. However, spot priming of repairs, such as filled nail holes, will still be necessary once the moulding is in place.

**Check the drying time**  Be sure to read the instructions on the primer tin to see when you can apply the finish coats. While the primer must have time to dry completely, it is also important to apply top coats as soon as possible after it is dry. A primer left uncovered for too long makes a poor surface for the paint.

**Painting woodwork**  When the primer is dry, sand lightly and wipe away the dust. Rub the surface of painted wood with a fine-grit sandpaper to provide a key for the new paint.

**Painting mouldings**  Work from a stepladder or platform if necessary. Start wherever you prefer, working from right to left if you are right-handed, or left to right if you are left-handed.

**Painting fitted furniture**  Bookcases, cabinets and other fitted furniture should receive the same preparation as other woodwork. Use a washable paint on these areas. If possible, remove shelves before painting, or follow the sequence on page 87.

**PRIMING WOOD**

**Apply in the direction of the grain**
Brush on primer with a 50mm (2in) brush, in the direction of the wood grain. Don't be concerned if the primer appears to be splodgy and uneven. The finishing coats of paint will smooth out the surface.

**AVOIDING MASKING**

Masking (*p.49*) takes a great deal of time. To avoid masking, hold a straight-edge in your free hand to protect adjacent surfaces as you paint. To paint the skirting board, hold the straight edge to protect the floor.

## PAINTING WOODWORK

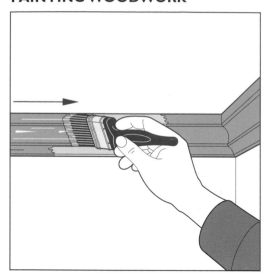

### Painting ceiling mouldings

Start in the corner, using a 50mm (2in) brush. Apply the paint in the direction of the wood grain. Brush out and smooth the paint without reloading. On the next section, apply the paint and brush it back towards the wet edge. Feather the edge of one section, before moving on to the next.

### Painting intricate mouldings

Use a stencil brush to fill the indentations in ornate mouldings. The round shape and closely spaced bristles of a stencil brush do a good job of forcing paint into every part of the design.

### ① Feather the edge

Lap marks show up more on glossy paint than on matt. Most woodwork is finished with a shiny surface, so it is important to feather the edge of each area of new paint. Brush the surface lightly with the tips of the bristles, lifting them at the edge of a newly painted area.

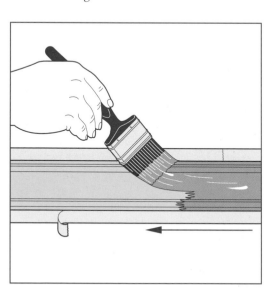

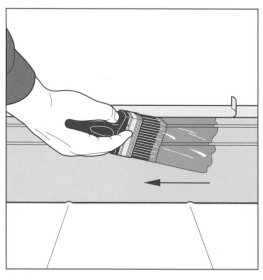

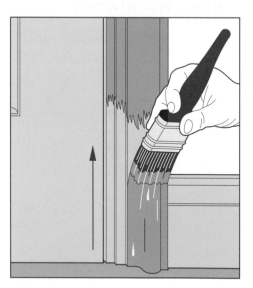

### Painting dado rails

Be sure to protect the wall on both sides of the rail. For the narrow edges along the top and bottom of the rail, use a small pad or a very narrow paint brush. Paint the edges while the main part of the rail is still wet. Smooth out drips before moving to another section.

### Painting skirting boards

As with other woodwork, apply the paint in the direction of the wood grain. Protect the floor with masking tape, heavy paper, or a straight-edge.

### ② Keep a wet edge on woodwork

Paint woodwork in small sections, keeping a wet edge to avoid lap marks. Apply new paint to a dry area and work back towards the previously applied paint. Brush in the direction of the grain.

## PAINTING FIXED SHELVES

**Treat each shelf as a separate section. Complete an entire section before moving on to the next.**

### WORK SEQUENCE

1 **Starting above the top shelf, paint the back wall of the bookcase.**
2 **Next, paint the side walls of the section you are working on.**
3 **Then paint the upper and lower shelf surfaces.**
4 **Complete the other sections in the same way.**
5 **Finally, paint the exposed horizontal and vertical edges.**

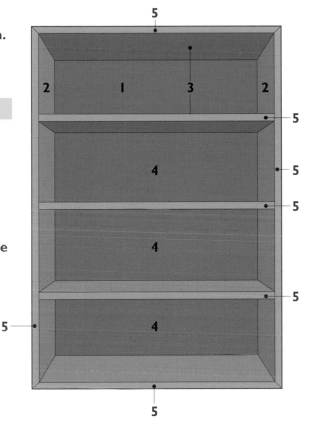

### PROFESSIONAL TIP

To paint removable shelves without touching the wet paint, take the shelves out and drive nails part of the way through their edges. Then rest the nails on trestles or old chairs (*p.89*), leaving the surface of the shelf clear for painting.

## STAINING WOODWORK

**1 Apply the stain**
Wear rubber gloves and protect the floor and walls by masking. Apply the stain with a brush or rag, following the direction of the wood grain. Work in small sections so that you can control the depth of stain penetration.

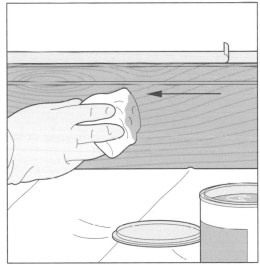

**2 Wipe off the stain**
To ensure an even finish, wait as directed on the label, then wipe off with a clean rag. As the work progresses, you will develop a sense of the time to wait between application and wiping off.

### STAINS

Stains add colour to wood, while allowing its natural grain pattern to show through. When staining, allow the liquid to seep into the wood and then wipe off the excess. By themselves, most stains do not protect the wood, and should be covered with polyurethane or another clear varnish. However, there are products available that contain both a stain and a protective finish.

The final look of the piece will depend on two things: the colour of the stain and your technique in applying it. Many shops have colour samples, or the colour may be shown on the tin. The final shade will depend on how long you allow the stain to penetrate the wood before wiping off the excess. Practise on a section of woodwork that will be hidden behind furniture, or on a matching piece of scrap wood.

# Doors

The typical home may have a number of different types of doors. They may be panelled or flush, hollow or solid-core, louvred or glazed, and may open by means of either hinges or runners. Although the painting technique differs for each type of door, the finish must withstand dirty hands, bumps and the occasional kick. You should, therefore, paint doors with satin or semi-gloss paint for maximum protection and easier cleaning (*see p.23*).

It is easier to paint a door in situ, than to take it off its hinges. However, if the door sticks when you open or close it, now may be a good time to take it down. Sometimes sticking is caused by the accumulation of layers of paint. Cure the problem by removing the door and sanding the paint off the edge that is sticking.

If the door is new, paint it before hanging it. Ask the manufacturer for advice on painting the top and bottom edges of the door. Generally, you should paint the bottoms of doors that open to the outside, and those which are exposed to wet floors. Only doors that open to the outside have their top edges painted.

**Removing door knobs on interior doors** Loosen the screws on the doorknobs. Then pull or unscrew the knob from the spindle.

> **PROFESSIONAL TIP**
>
> If you are painting the door in situ, hold it open with a rolled-up newspaper or some other type of wedge. Place a dust sheet or newspapers under the door to catch any drips.

## PREPARING DOORS

**① Remove doorknobs**
Remove the screw that holds the knob to the spindle, then remove the knob. The protective plate around the spindle should then slip off, unless it is held in place by a screw. Remove the screws from the latch plate and then pull out the assembly.

**② Mask round the doors**
When painting doors, follow the directions for masking (*p.49*) and protect surrounding walls with masking tape. Make sure that the door is firmly wedged open.

## REMOVING HINGE PINS

**①** **Take the door off its hinges**
To remove most doors, unscrew the screws that attach the hinges to the door. However, if the door is hung on loose-pin butt hinges, the pins can be removed with a screwdriver and hammer (*see above*).

**②** **If a hinge pin won't budge**
If a hinge pin won't budge, blunt the end of a 50mm (2in) nail and insert it in the bottom of the hinge barrel. Tap the nail head with a hammer until the pin pops free.

## REMOVING PAINT BUILDUP

Remove the door from its hinges and stand it on its edge. Scrape off the old paint with a putty knife or an old chisel. Follow with a coarse-grit sandpaper and then a finer-grit paper, until the edge is smooth. Then paint the door and replace it.

## PAINTING REMOVED DOORS

**Lay the door across trestles**
If you are removing the door, lay it across two trestles for painting. Cover the tops of the trestles with old towels to protect the door. Paint one side of the door (*p.90*), wait until it is dry, turn the door over, and then paint the other side.

**An alternative method**
To paint the second side before the first is dry, drive two nails into the top and bottom edges of the door before you start to paint. Rest the nails on trestles. With a helper, hold the nails and turn the door over. Do not use this method on very heavy doors.

### FIXING DOORS THAT STICK

There are many reasons why doors stick. The screws in the hinges may be loose, so check, and tighten them, if necessary. If the bottom of the door scrapes against the floor, you should trim it. To trim the door accurately, first mark the area of the door that scrapes. Then remove the door from its hinges. Plane it with a small block plane or a power plane. Do not plane beyond the marked area. Finally, paint the door before you replace it.

## PAINTING DOORS

Since a door is such a visible part of any room, take pains to apply a smooth, even finish. Help prevent lap marks by painting the entire door in one session. Begin by preparing the surface of the door as shown on pages 81–84. Prime as needed.

**Painting each side a different colour** Most people paint doors the same colour as the rest of the woodwork in the room. If the door separates two rooms with different-coloured woodwork, each side is painted the appropriate colour, and the latch edge is painted the same colour as the room into which the door opens.

Simple enough, but what guides your colour selection if the door is usually kept open? The best solution is to paint the door a separate accent colour that will harmonise with the colour in the adjoining room.

---

**PROFESSSIONAL TIP**

When you paint a door in situ, leave enough time to paint the doorjambs and the hinge edge of the door first. Allow them to dry before painting the face and the latch edge of the door. You can then half-close the door without spoiling the finish on the inside jamb. Also, you won't ruin the finish, or your clothes, if you should accidently brush against the latch jamb.

---

## FLUSH DOORS

**Generally, flush doors offer a solid, unbroken surface for painting. They can be of either solid-core or hollow-core construction.**

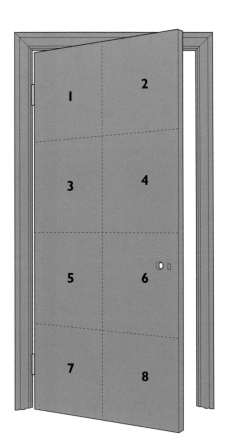

---

### WORK SEQUENCE

1  **Start in the upper left corner and paint an area extending about half the way across the top of the door and a quarter of the way down.**

2  **Paint the adjoining top section.**
3  **Follow the sequence shown on the diagram (*left*) to finish the door.**

### PAINTING FLUSH DOORS

**Lay on the paint**
Load the bottom third of the bristles on a 75mm (3in) brush with paint. Start at the top of the door near the corner and paint the first section. Smooth the paint with horizontal strokes, then finish in the direction of the wood grain.

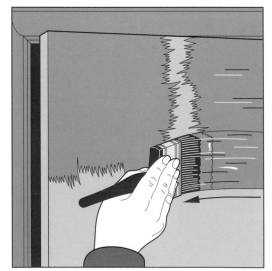

**Feather the edge**
Follow the instructions for feathering on page 38. Begin painting the second portion of the door on a dry section and work towards the wet paint. Smooth out any drips and beads that form along the edges, top and bottom of the door.

## USING A ROLLER

With a little practice, a roller will help you to make short work of flush doors.

**Start in the middle**
Work from the middle of the door to the top. Apply paint over the entire top half of the door. Reload the roller and apply paint over the bottom half.

## PANELLED DOORS

Panelled doors have a more distinctive appearance than flush doors and require a little more care when painting. To paint panel doors proceed as follows:

### WORK SEQUENCE

1   Paint the panels first.
2   Next, paint the central vertical stile if there is one.
3   Paint the top horizontal rail.
4   Paint the middle horizontal rail.
5   Paint the other stiles.
6   Finally, paint the bottom horizontal rail of the door.

## PAINTING A PANELLED DOOR

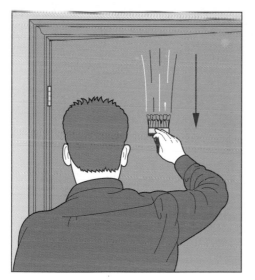

**Smooth with a brush**
Use a brush to smooth out the finish. Paint from the top of the door down, in long, even strokes.

**Painting the panels**
Load a 50mm (2in) brush with paint and begin on the moulding that surrounds one of the panels. Then paint the panel. Brush paint across the grain for even coverage, but always end by brushing in the direction of the grain.

**Painting the stiles and rails**
Once you have painted the panels, paint the rest of the door in the sequence shown in the diagram above. Paint in the direction of the wood grain. Work quickly. You should aim to complete the door while all the paint is still wet.

## SLIDING DOORS

**Sliding doors and French windows should be painted in the same way as any other type of door. The important difference is that these doors usually have glass panels that must be protected from paint. Mask as necessary. Paint the outside as well as the inside. Paint sliding doors in a clockwise direction as follows:**

### WORK SEQUENCE

1  **Begin by painting the left-hand vertical edge.**
2  **Paint the top of the frame.**
3  **Go on to the other side and the bottom of the same door.**
4  **Move on to the other door and repeat the sequence.**

### PROFESSIONAL TIP

Keep the sliding section of the door open an inch or two until the paint dries thoroughly. If you close the door while the paint is still wet, it will stick. Also, move the slider occasionally to prevent the paint from forming a seal where the door meets the top and bottom tracks.

## LOUVRE DOORS

**Louvre doors are usually found on cupboards, and on most, the slats are fixed. Since the aim is to completely cover the slats, paint the inside of the door first. This also helps you to catch any paint drips from the front. Experiment using a foam pad (*p.29*) to paint the slats.**

**To paint louvre doors proceed as follows:**

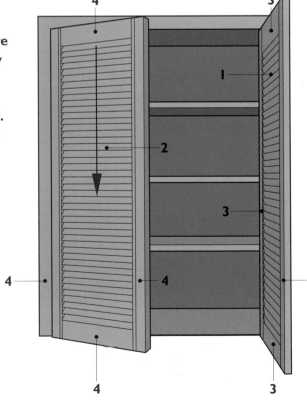

### WORK SEQUENCE

1  **Paint the inside of the louvred section of the door. Work on one slat at a time, from the top down. (The method for painting each slat is shown on page 93.)**
2  **Repeat the process on the outside of the door.**
3  **Then paint the top, sides and bottom on the inside of the door.**
4  **Finally, paint the top, sides and bottom of the outside of the door.**

## PAINTING SLATS ON FIXED LOUVRES

### SPRAY PAINTING LOUVRE DOORS

One way to ensure total coverage of door louvres, is to use a spray. Take the door off its hinges and carry it outside. Stand it against a wall or lay it over trestles. Be sure the area behind the door is protected from paint which may spray through the open louvres.

Begin by painting the back of the door, applying the paint in even strokes, and keeping the sprayer nozzle at a right angle to the surface (*p.42*).

**① Work the paint into the crevices**
Using a 25mm (1in) brush, work the paint into the crevices between the slats of the louvre. Paint from one edge towards the centre of the slat. Be sure to paint the edge of the frame that holds the slats, but do not allow paint to accumulate there.

**② Brush the paint back**
Flow the paint onto the wood in a long, smooth stroke. Start the next stroke at the opposite end of the same slat and flow the paint towards the wet area. Then smooth out the paint with one stroke across the slat. Move on to the next slat down.

## PAINTING ADJUSTABLE LOUVRES

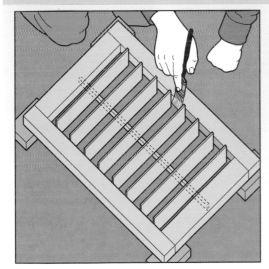

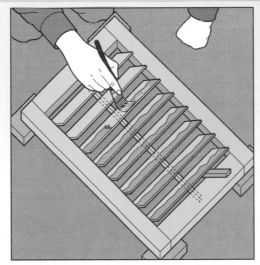

**① Paint the edges of the frame**
Open the louvres wide so that the slats are set horizontally. On the side of the door opposite the adjusting rod, use a 25mm (1in) brush to paint the inside edges of the frame where it meets the slats.

**② Paint both sides of the slats**
Wedge a stick between the first slat and the frame and paint the tops of both sides of the slats. Remove the stick, close the slats and finish the unpainted areas of slats. Then paint the frame.

**③ Paint the other side of the door**
On the other side of the door, paint the unpainted areas on the slats and the adjusting rod. Then paint the frame.

# Windows

Windows come in a variety of shapes, sizes and materials. Directions for preparing and painting sash, casement and top-hinged windows are shown on the following pages. For other types, such as fixed, bow and garden windows, follow the lead illustrated in the process for painting the three main window types: start by painting along the edge nearest the glass and work out to the architraves.

We will deal primarily with paintable wooden window frames here, but your windows may have PVC, aluminium or glass-fibre frames. They may even have frames made of two materials, such as wood with a cladding that you do not have to paint.

As with other woodwork, window frames should be painted with a gloss paint to protect the surface and make them easier to clean. When you are working, take care not to make the common error of smearing paint onto the glass. Painting the window frames in the proper sequence (*see pp.96,98*) will help to prevent this. Allow the paint to dry completely before closing the windows.

**Opening a window that sticks** There are several ways to open a stuck window. But there is a wrong way – the method that results in breaking the glass. Whichever technique you try, proceed slowly and carefully. Start with the simplest solution and work your way up to the most drastic (*see p.95*).

**Preparing window frames** Clean window frames with a household cleaner to remove dirt and grease. Don't bother to clean the glass until you have finished painting.

**Preparing new windows** Sand the rough spots on unpainted window frames and wipe with a tack cloth or a damp rag. Allow to dry thoroughly. Apply a coat of primer to seal the surface. Sand and paint when this is dry (*see pp.97–99*).

**Cleaning the surface** Wipe down all the wood with a tack cloth or a damp rag to remove sanding dust. Allow the surface to dry before painting.

**Protecting the glass** It is best to mask the glass when you are painting window frames (*see p.49*). However, with a little practice and concentration, it is possible to paint without masking. If you do not mask, keep a clean rag handy for removing any wet paint from the glass.

## REPLACING BROKEN GLASS

To replace broken glass properly, wear protective gloves and follow these basic steps:

- Remove all broken glass and buy a new sheet that is 3mm ($\frac{1}{8}$in) smaller in length and width than the opening.
- Use a wire brush to clean out the rebate (notch) that held the glass.
- Apply primer to the rebate and allow it to dry.
- Roll out a thin bead of putty and place it in the rebate. The compound will act as a bed for the new glass. Set the glass in place.
- Position glazing sprigs against the glass and force them into the wood with a pin hammer. Insert a sprig every 250mm (10in) along the edge of the glass.
- Roll some putty into a rope and press it against the edge of the glass. Starting in a corner, take a completely clean putty knife, hold it at about a 40° angle, and smooth out the putty until you reach another corner. Work in one continuous motion. Carefully scrape away any left-over putty. Leave the putty for about two weeks to harden slightly before painting it.

## OPENING A SASH WINDOW THAT STICKS

### Use a screwdriver

If a sash-cord window is stuck with paint, insert a long screwdriver into the sash-cord channel and rock it back and forth. This may break the paint seal.

### Cut the paint with a knife

An alternative method for opening a stuck window is to cut through the paint seal with a sharp knife. Take care to cut only the dry paint and not to gouge the wood of the window frame.

### Use a putty knife and hammer

If the screwdriver and knife fail, work the corner of a putty knife between the sash and the staff bead that holds it in place. Insert as much of the blade as possible. Tap gently with a hammer to make an opening. Repeat the process all the way round the frame.

### Remove the sash bead

A final solution calls for the removal of the staff bead. Cut through the paint along the side of the bead with a sharp knife, and prise it off with a small crowbar. Use a piece of folded cardboard or a wood block to protect the architrave.

**PROFESSIONAL TIP**

The best brush to use on window frames is an angled cutting-in brush. With the bristles forming an angle, you can get the paint into corners and you'll find it easy to use on the frame's many narrow surfaces.

**PROFESSIONAL TIP**

If you are not masking when painting window frames, you can allow a thin line of paint, about 3mm ($1/8$in) wide, to overlap the glass. It will help keep moisture from working its way between the putty and the glass.

## PREPARING WINDOWS FOR PAINTING

**1 Remove the hardware**
Remove all hardware, such as handles and locks, and place them in a plastic bag. If they are covered with old paint, soak the parts in the appropriate solvent (p.30) to remove the paint.

**2 Fill any holes**
Use putty or wood filler to fill all holes in the wood. Apply it with a putty knife, and smooth it level with the surface of the wood. Allow to dry thoroughly. Sand, if necessary, and spot prime.

**3 Sand painted windows**
Use a fine-grit sandpaper to roughen the surfaces of painted window frames (p.84). Tear the paper into thin strips for sanding the mullions. Alternatively, you could use sugar soap to dull the sheen.

## SASH WINDOWS

**Before beginning to paint a sash window, pull down the outer sash and lift the inner sash.**

### WORK SEQUENCE

1  Paint the outer glazing bars.
2  Paint the bottom and as much of the sides of the outer sash as you can reach.
3  Reverse the sash positions. Paint the rest of the outer sash.
4  Paint the inner sash.
5  When the paint is dry, push both sashes down and paint the upper jambs. When they are dry, push the sashes up and paint the lower jambs. Then paint the frame.

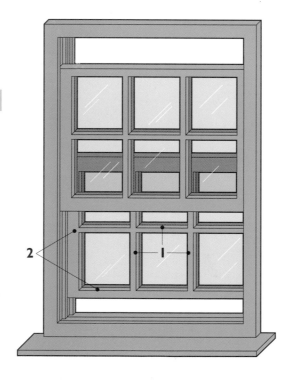

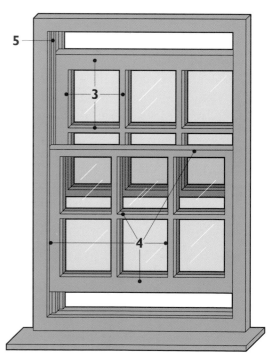

## PAINTING SASH WINDOWS

**1 Paint the glazing bars**
Push the inner sash up and lower the outer sash. Paint the glazing bars on the outer sash. Hold the brush as you would a pencil. With the longest bristles uppermost, flex the bristles against the wood and draw the brush along the bar/glass edge.

**2 Paint the bottom and sides of the outer sash**
Next paint the bottom and sides of the outer sash. Paint as far up the sides of the sash as you can reach.

**3 Reverse the sashes**
Move the inner sash down to within 25mm (1in) of being closed and raise the outer sash to about 25mm (1in) from the top. Paint the rest of the outer sash.

**4 Paint the inner sash**
Paint the entire inner sash. Do not close the sashes until the paint is dry. While the paint is drying, move the sashes up and down slightly from time to time to prevent a paint seal from forming.

**5 Paint the jambs**
When the sashes are completely dry (wait at least 24 hours), push both all the way down. Paint the upper half of the jambs. Allow to dry completely, then push the sashes up and paint the lower half. Paint the staff beads, then paint the frame.

### PAINTING WINDOW JAMBS

Paint the lower window jambs the same colour as the interior woodwork. Paint the upper jambs the same colour as the exterior woodwork. This ensures a uniform colour, whether the window is open or closed, and whether it is viewed from the inside or the outside of the house.

## CASEMENT WINDOWS

To paint a casement window proceed as follows:

### WORK SEQUENCE

1 **Open the window and paint the edge of the frame where it meets the glass.**
2 **Paint the top of the window.**
3 **Then paint the bottom and sides of the window.**
4 **Paint the window jambs.**
5 **Finally, paint the window frame.**

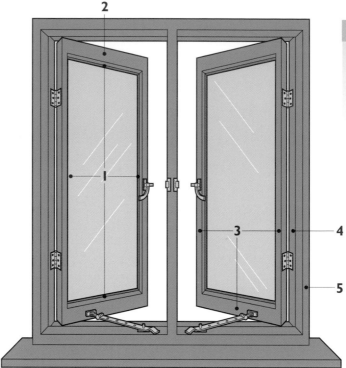

### PROFESSIONAL TIP

**Metal Windows**
Clean the windows and remove rust with a wire brush. Prime with a metal primer before painting. Paint as shown on pages 97–99.

### PROFESSIONAL TIP

Many painters get good results by using a small roller, or a painting pad, rather than a brush on window frames. Use a roller on the wider areas of the frame. Painting pads have tapered edges that do a good job on glazing bars. Pads work well with water-based paints, but some oil-based paints may damage them.

## PAINTING CASEMENT WINDOWS

**Paint the casement**
Open the window and begin at the top of the casement. Start by painting the edge along the glass and, working outwards, paint in the direction of the wood grain. Paint the bottom and sides. On multipane windows, paint the glazing bars first.

**Paint the jambs**
Paint the jambs when the casement has had time to dry. While the paint is drying, open and close the window a little to break any paint seal that may form. Avoid getting paint on the hinges.

## TOP-HINGED WINDOWS

This type of window is similar to a casement turned on its side. Paint in the same manner as for a casement.

### WORK SEQUENCE

1 Open the window and paint the edge of the frame where it meets the glass.
2 Paint the top of the window.
3 Then paint the bottom and sides of the window.
4 Paint the window jambs.
5 Finally, paint the window frame.

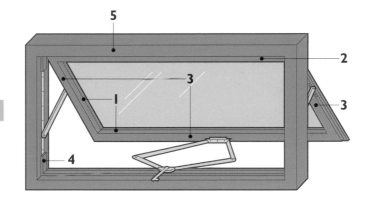

### REMOVING PAINT FROM GLASS

- Use a clean cloth to wipe up any paint that finds its way onto the glass.
- Wrap a cloth round the blade of a putty knife to clean paint from the edges of the glass.

- If you miss some spots, leave the paint until it is dry to the touch, then scrape it off with a glass scraper.

### TO AVOID MASKING WINDOW PANES

**1 Overlap the glass with paint**
Rather than masking, allow your brush to overlap the glass slightly. Keep the overlap small and concentrate on applying the paint smoothly over the frame. Wait until the paint is dry to the touch, but not cured completely.

**2 Score the paint**
At this stage, the paint will still be wet, but you won't be able to smudge it with your finger. Using a straight-edge and a sharp knife, score a line through the paint on the glass about 3mm ($^1$/8in) from the frame.

**3 Scrape away the excess**
Using a glass scraper, scrape the paint from the glass up to the score line. This should provide the window frame with a crisp painted edge. Allow the paint to dry completely before you clean the windows.

Painted finishes on walls and cabinets can enhance and soften the hard metal and tile surfaces usually found in kitchens and bathrooms. But because these rooms get a lot of use and, inevitably, collect grease and dirt, the paint must be both washable and impervious to the water vapour generated by cooking and bathing.

# CHAPTER 7

# KITCHENS AND BATHROOMS

# The surfaces

Begin by doing the preparatory work you would do in any other room: scrape loose paint and repair damage to walls and ceilings (*see pp.58–68*). Thorough cleaning of the walls and other surfaces is especially important here. In some cases you may have to scrape away layers of grease or soap film that have built up in out-of-the-way spots. Check behind the cooker and on the walls round extractor hoods and fans. Be sure to remove all the grease, otherwise, the paint will not adhere to the surface.

You must also decide if you want to paint the cabinets in these rooms. If they are in good condition and will blend with the new colour scheme, it is probably best to leave them as they are. Just make sure they are well protected while you paint. You can either paint or replace any damaged or shabby cabinets.

New cabinets enhance the appearance of the room and they may provide you with more storage space than the existing ones. However, new cabinets can be expensive. So, if it is the finish you want to change, and not the insides of the cabinets, consider painting or staining them. A new colour, along with some new handles and knobs for all the cabinets and drawers, will refresh and update even the shabbiest kitchen.

When choosing a colour for the cabinets, remember that it will set the tone for the entire room. A very fashionable colour may soon become dated. Applying a neutral colour will allow something else to become the focal point of the room.

## MATERIALS AND TOOLS

**Cleaners**
**Sponges and non-scratch scouring pads**
**Paint scrapers**
**Plasterboard saw**
**Sandpaper**
**Screwdriver**
**Masking tape**
**Dust sheets (fabric and plastic)**
**Brushes and rollers**
**Primer**
**Paint**

## IMPROVING VENTILATION

The moisture that builds up in kitchens and bathrooms should be vented out. Water vapour that condenses on walls and other surfaces can lead to peeling paint, mildew and, in extreme cases, structural damage. Most new houses have some kind of mechanical ventilation, but older ones often do not. In addition to a window, a kitchen should have an extractor fan mounted in a cooker hood. A bathroom should have one installed in the wall or the ceiling. Models are available that include both a light fitting and an extractor. Consult a contractor who specialises in kitchens and bathrooms for advice on choosing and installing an extractor fan.

# Kitchens

**Protecting kitchens** When you set out to paint your kitchen, you will notice how little of the room needs to be painted. This means there are far more surfaces, including worktops, appliances and cabinets, to protect from splattered paint.

**Covering appliances** Move appliances, with the exception of the cooker, to the centre of the room and cover them with dust sheets. You should also cover the floor with dust sheets.

**Removing hardware** Cabinet and drawer handles can be removed by unscrewing them from the inside. Place all hardware and screws in a plastic bag until it is time to replace them.

**Cleaning walls** Clean off grease with either a household detergent or sugar soap. A sponge, or non-abrasive scouring pad will clean off grime. Remove mould with a solution of 0.57 litres (1 pint) of chlorine bleach to 5.7 litres (10 pints) of water.

**Work areas** If the kitchen is small, you may need to use a worktop or a tabletop as your work area for mixing and pouring paint. Cover the surface with dust sheets and, to protect it against paint tin scratches, use a few layers of old newspapers too.

## MOVING LARGE APPLIANCES

Kitchens usually contain large appliances and, sometimes, large pieces of furniture, such as dressers, that must be moved away from the walls. Since these items are usually heavy and awkward, walk them, rather than lift them. Begin by moving one corner of the appliance a short distance and then do the same to the opposite corner. Although this method takes time, you will avoid injuring yourself. Protect your floor from scratches by walking heavy appliances onto pieces of thick cardboard or a piece of old carpeting turned upside down.

## PREPARING KITCHENS

**Move appliances away from the walls**
Where appliances can't be placed in the centre of the room, because the room is small or has a central island, move the cooker and refrigerator far enough away from the wall to let you to paint behind them.

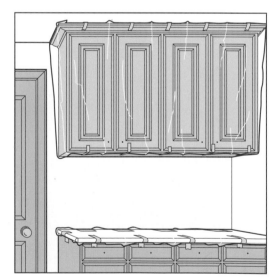

**Protect the cabinets**
If you are not going to paint the cabinets, hang a sheet of plastic over them. Secure it with masking tape at the top and sides. If you do plan to paint them later, don't bother masking them. Cover worktops, too.

## PAINTING KITCHEN CEILINGS AND WALLS

Before painting unpainted walls and ceilings, you must apply a coat of primer (*see p.24*). Previously painted walls do not need priming if you have removed all the grease. If you aren't certain that the surfaces are absolutely free of dirt, apply a primer.

Use a high sheen paint such as a semigloss that can stand up to repeated washing. Many manufacturers have introduced paints that are specially formulated for use in kitchens and bathrooms. These products contain a fungicide that will help to prevent mildew from forming on the finish. They can also withstand the high moisture levels in these rooms.

Paint in the same order as for any other room: first the ceiling, then the walls, the woodwork and, finally, the cabinets.

## PAINTING KITCHEN CABINETS

There are two decisions you must make before painting kitchen cabinets: should you paint the insides of the cabinets; and should the doors be left on or taken off?

Unless the cabinets have glass doors, don't bother to paint them inside. Kitchen cabinets are usually closed, and when they are open whatever is stored inside them usually hides the walls. With base units you must bend over or squat down to see inside. Of course, it may bother you to see unpainted interiors every time you open a cabinet door. If you decide to paint them, follow the painting sequence on page 104.

If you are considering whether to remove the cabinet doors, follow these basic guidelines:

- Don't remove the doors if you are simply going to sand and paint them, unless you find it easier to remove the doors than to paint round the exposed hinges.
- Remove the doors if you plan to install new exposed hinges.
- Remove the doors if you are going to strip the old finish. This will allow you to apply the stripper outdoors. Follow the directions for stripping woodwork on pages 82–83.

Make sure that you get a good finish on your old cabinets by choosing the best-quality primer and paint available. It is also a good idea to use new brushes and to invest in tack cloths for removing sanding dust.

Prepare kitchen cabinets carefully before painting them. Use a fine-grit sandpaper to sand the the doors and drawers. Then sand the frame of the cabinet. This removes imperfections and provides a good base for the primer. Wipe up the sanding dust with a tack cloth or a damp rag. Then apply a coat of primer.

### SAFETY FOR GAS COOKERS

Always be careful if you have to move a gas cooker. You will be unable to move a cooker that is connected to the gas supply by a rigid pipe. If the cooker is attached by flexible tubing, use a torch to see how much slack there is behind the appliance. It is better to leave the cooker in place than to risk stretching the tubing too far. If the wall behind or beside the cooker is visible and must be painted, use a small roller attached to an extension handle.

The main consideration for any kitchen is that it should be both functional and bright. This is why one of the most popular colours for kitchens has been white with a contrasting colour like blue or yellow. Nowadays, however, many people are choosing more dramatic or fashionable colours to make the colour scheme in the kitchen just as interesting as in the other rooms in a house. These colours often work well because, if you choose bland, neutral colours, you may well find that such objects as a refrigerator and a cooking range may seem to dominate the room.

## KITCHEN CABINETS

**If you want to paint the insides of a cabinet, follow the sequence shown on page 87. If you want to paint only the outside, proceed as follows:**

1  **Paint the inside then the outside of the doors.**
2  **Next, paint the horizontal sections of the frame.**
3  **Then paint the vertical sections, or stiles, of the frame.**
4  **Finally, conclude by painting the outsides of the cabinet.**

## PAINTING UNDER WALL CABINETS

**1 Cut in under the cabinet**
Use a 50mm (2in) brush to cut in under the cabinet. In most cases, you will be able to use the bottom edge of a wall cabinet as a guide. Painting this area can be awkward as you must bend and reach across the worktop to get to the wall.

**2 Lay on, smooth the paint and feather the edge**
Cover the rest of the area with a 75mm (3in) brush. Then lay on and smooth the paint and feather the edge (*p.38*). Work in sections that span the distance between the bottom of the cabinet and the worktop.

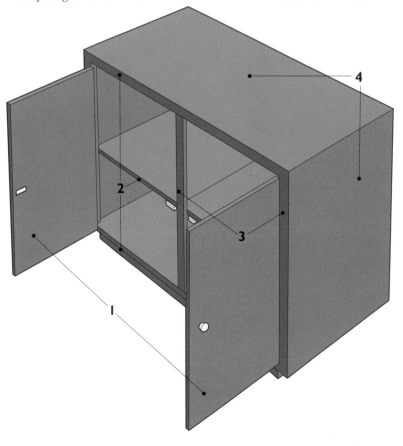

## PAINTING KITCHEN CABINETS

### 1 Paint the doors
Use a new 75mm (3in) brush to paint the inside of the door, using your free hand to hold the door steady. Don't forget to paint the hinge edge of the door. Allow the paint to dry before closing the door, then paint the outside of the door.

### 2 Paint the horizontal sections
Use a 50mm (2in) brush to paint the horizontal sections of the cabinet frame. Don't forget to include the front of the cabinet shelves.

### 3 Paint the vertical sections
Next, paint the vertical sections of the cabinet. Be sure to go over your work and correct any paint drips or runs that may have occurred.

### 4 Paint the sides
Finish by painting any exposed sides of the cabinet. These usually occur where neighbouring cabinets are of different depths, or at the end of a run of cabinets.

### GETTING NEW HARDWARE
Consider installing new cabinet hardware to finish the job. Replace handles with handles and knobs with knobs because their holes are already in place. If you change the style of the hardware, fill any unwanted holes before painting, and drill new ones after painting. Use a spirit level when you fit the new handles.

# Bathrooms

**Preparing bathrooms** Unlike the other rooms in the house, bathrooms rarely have movable furniture, and most pieces will need to be protected as directed below. Any furniture that can be moved should be removed and stored elsewhere until the job is completed.

Scrape loose paint and make any repairs to walls and woodwork, as necessary. If mildew is present, remove it with a solution of one part chlorine bleach to ten parts water.

**Painting bathrooms** A high-sheen paint will make the bathroom easier to clean. Also, you could consider using paint that is made specially for bathrooms.

**Choosing painted or tiled surfaces** Ceramic tiles, which can be washed down easily, may seem to be a good solution for bathrooms (and many kitchens). However, bathrooms (and some kitchens), tend to have recesses, ledges and pipes that cannot be tiled. It is best to paint these areas, especially as there are now paints on the market that are formulated to cope with high-moisture conditions.

## DEALING WITH WATER DAMAGE

Water damage in bathrooms can be caused by leaky pipes, spray from showers, or condensation. To avoid further damage, deal with the source of the problem before you begin to paint (*p.59*). Deal with water spots by priming the affected area with a coating that contains shellac.

## MAINTAINING THE FINISH

Keep your paintwork looking like new by ensuring proper ventilation in the room. If necessary, wipe down walls with a dry cloth or towel to remove condensation.

Regularly clean soap scum off the walls with a bathroom cleaner.

### Protect parts of the bathroom that won't be painted

Cover up any unpainted areas of the bathroom, such as the pedestal and wash-hand basin, with dust sheets. Tape plastic sheets over tiles. Use dust sheets on the floor. Protect the bath by taping a dust sheet over it.

## PROTECTING BATHROOM FIXTURES

## PROTECTING BATHROOM FITTINGS

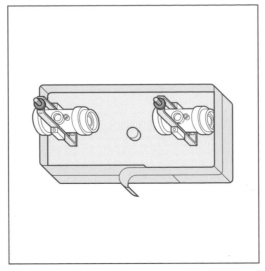

**PROFESSIONAL TIP**

When painting the walls of a small bathroom, save time on each wall by cutting in along the ceiling and around bathroom cabinets, windows and doors all at once. Since each wall will cover such a small area, you should be able to avoid lap marks by painting the walls before the borders dry.

### Cover the taps
Keep paint drips and splatters off taps by making hoods from newspapers. First, fold a sheet of paper into a semi-circle and then attach it to the wall with masking tape.

### Protect the light fittings
Remove the shade and bulb. Apply masking tape round the edges of the fitting. For extra light while you are working, keep light bulbs in place on the opposite wall.

## PAINTING BATHROOMS

### Painting round the bathroom cabinet
Mask the edges of the cabinet with masking tape, then use a 50mm (2in) brush to apply the paint. Paint round the cabinet in the same way that you would paint round a window. Keep a clean cloth handy to wipe up any paint splatters on the cabinet.

### Painting round a light fitting
Use a 50mm (2in) brush to paint round a light fitting. If you had the light on when painting other parts of the room, switch it off and remove the bulbs now. If you keep them in place, their glare will prevent you from seeing what you are painting.

### Clean up splashes on tiles
Wipe up splashes immediately. If you miss any, let them dry completely, then rub off with a nonscratch scouring pad.

Some areas of the home present special challenges and need to be dealt with differently from the rest of the painting project. In this chapter you'll find directions for refinishing floors and painting stairs, stairwells, pipes and masonry. These areas are important parts of your home and should be given the same attention as walls and ceilings. You will learn how to tackle these jobs and achieve good results.

**CHAPTER 8**

# SPECIAL SITUATIONS

# Stairs and stairwells

Although they may not take up a great deal of space, staircases and stairwells require special attention. A staircase may be the focal point in a house. Even a house that has little ornamentation elsewhere may have an attractive staircase. Thus, the stairs should be restored and painted with care.

In most houses the stairs are in almost constant use, so it is important to learn how to paint them while allowing people to use them. This will require careful timing, and the work must be carried out in a specific sequence.

**Staining or painting**  In many older homes, stairs were constructed from high-quality woods that were stained rather than painted. If your stairs are painted but the house has ornate mouldings in other areas, the stairs may have decorative elements too, and it may be worthwhile stripping and staining them (*see p.82*). Choose an inconspicuous part of the stairs and scrape off the paint. If there is a build-up of layers of old paint, you will need to use a chemical stripper to remove the finish down to the bare wood. A carpenter should be able to identify the wood and advise you on the feasibility of stripping all the stairs. It may not be worth stripping and staining stairs if they are made of low-quality wood.

**Choosing paint**  It is usually best to choose for a staircase wall the same paint sheen you selected for other walls in the house. But consider using a more washable sheen if the staircase walls have become dirty because people touch them when they use the stairs. You can avoid this problem and increase safety by installing a handrail on the wall.

**Special equipment**  The high walls and ceilings of stairwells present their own set of challenges. You will need a special ladder and a platform when painting stairwells (*see p.111*). Retractable stepladders allow you to adjust the height of each leg independently for setting up on stairs. You may also need a straight ladder, of the type that is usually used for outdoor work, to anchor one side of the platform. A roller extension will also help you to reach the ceiling and the tops of the high walls in a stairwell.

## MATERIALS AND TOOLS

**Stains and paints**
**Ladders**
**Stepladders**
**Platform planks**
**Brushes, rollers and roller extensions**
**Heavy paper or masking tape**

## WORKING ON STAIRCASES

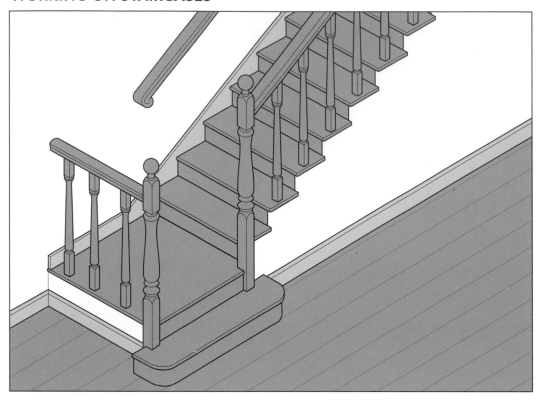

### The parts of a staircase

Even if the steps are covered with carpeting, you will still need to paint the stairwell and the balustrade, which includes the newel post, handrail and balusters of the railing. If you are adding a new railing, consider the reach of the elderly and children when deciding on the height of the handrail. One option is to install two handrails at different heights, to accommodate everyone in the family.

> **PROFESSIONAL TIP**
>
> As an alternative to the method shown below, paint alternate steps. Allow to dry, then paint the other steps. This will prevent lap marks.

## PAINTING STAIRCASES

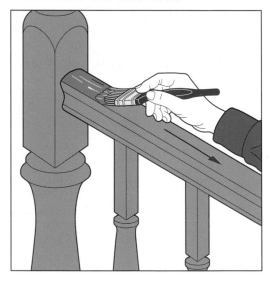

**1 Paint the handrail first**
Place dust sheets on the steps to protect against spills and begin by painting the balustrade. Use a narrow brush to apply paint or stain in the direction of the wood grain. Start at the top of the handrail and work downwards.

**2 Paint the balusters**
After masking round the base of the balusters with masking tape, paint the balusters. Brush from the bottom upwards. Smooth out the paint on each baluster to remove drips before moving on. Replace the tape when it begins to pick up paint.

**3 Paint the steps**
If the stairs are in use while you are painting, paint half the width of each step and allow to dry. Paint the riser and the tread of each step, then paint the overhang. When the painted portion is dry, paint the other half of each step.

## WORKING IN STAIRWELLS

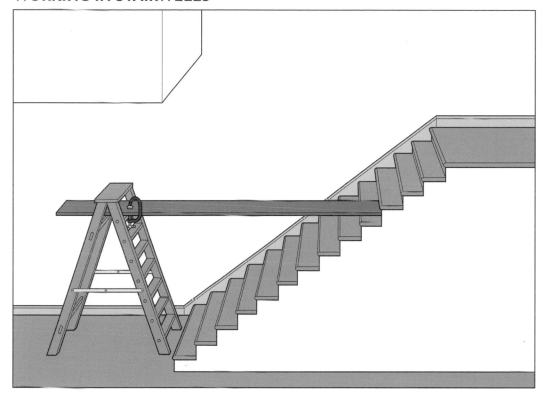

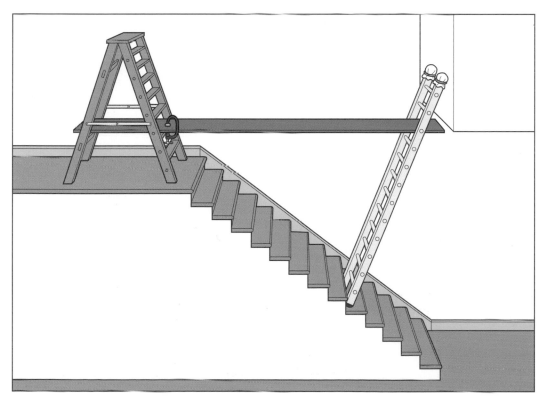

### Platforms for the lower stairwell

For lower areas, you may be able to use a platform with only a stepladder. Place the platform between the stepladder in the hall and one of the steps on the staircase. As you paint, move the platform down the stepladder rungs and the staircase steps.

### PROFESSIONAL TIP

Make sure that your platform is safe before you use it. The steps of the ladder should face towards the platform. This will provide the platform with adequate support. Clamp the platform to the ladder. Also, check the stepladder braces from time to time to make sure that they are locked and tight.

### Platforms for the upper stairwell

For high areas you will need a straight ladder and a stepladder. Place the platform between the stepladder at the top of the staircase and the straight ladder that is propped up against the wall. You can prevent the straight ladder from marking the wall by wrapping the top of it in a towel or by placing special rubber pads over the ends. To make it safe, the platform should overlap the ladder rungs by at least 300mm (12 in).

# Floors

Almost every kind of floor covering can be painted. This section deals with preparing, painting and refinishing wood floors, and preparing and painting concrete floors.

Use only those paints that have been specially designed for covering floors. Standard paints cannot withstand the amount of wear and tear that floors have to undergo. Floor paints are available in both solvent-based and water-based formulations.

Wood floors can be stained to allow the grain of the wood to show through and then covered with a clear protective finish. There are two main types of finishes: wax finishes and clear varnishes. The most popular clear varnishes are solvent-based polyurethanes and water-based acrylics. They are relatively easy to apply and are available in a variety of sheens. Nowadays, few people opt for a wax finish, but you may have to deal with a wax finish when stripping or repairing an old floor.

Whatever finish you decide on for your floor, you should begin the project by preparing the surface properly. You may need to make repairs and you will have to strip off the old finish before applying paint or varnish.

## MATERIALS AND TOOLS

**Paints and primers**
**Clear finishes**
**Stain and thinners**
**Rollers, roller extensions, brushes and paint pads**
**Fine wire wool**
**Crowbar**
**Hammer and nail punch**
**Power screwdriver**
**Carpenter's glue**
**Chisel**
**Sanding machines**
**Rotary buffing machines**
**Hand-held scrapers**
**Sandpaper**
**Buffing pads**
**Patching concrete**

## REPAIRING DAMAGED FINISHES

A wood floor that is showing its age because of damage or wear should be completely refinished or repainted. If the scuffs and scratches are not severe, you may be able to make spot repairs and prolong the life of the existing finish.

To find out which type of finish is on the floor, conduct a simple test. A wax finish will smudge when you press against it with your finger. You should also be able to remove some wax by scraping the surface with the edge of a coin. If the surface flakes up in pieces rather than producing a waxy residue, the finish is varnish.

If you have to repair an area that has been coloured with a stain, choose a stain that matches the colour of the rest of the floor most closely. Use a piece of wood of the same type as your floor to experiment with different ratios of stain to thinner until you match the colour most satisfactorily.

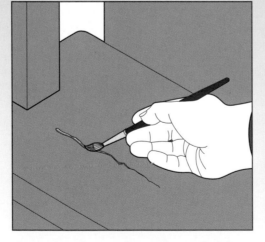

**Scratches in a polyurethane finish**
Using a finish that matches the existing sheen, apply polyurethane varnish with a paint brush. Wipe up varnish that drips onto other parts of the floor. You can buy kits for small repairs on this type of finish.

**Scratches in a wax finish**
First of all, buff the scratched area with a clean cloth. If the damage is still there, buff once more with extra-fine wire wool, then apply a light coating of wax to the damaged area and buff again.

## STAIN OR PAINT?

The natural grain of wood has an attractive pattern that is generally allowed to show through the finish of a wood floor. Usually, wood floors are treated with a light stain or left natural, with a clear, protective finish completing the job. But there are some situations when you may consider painting over a natural wood floor. A rich, opaque colour may suit your overall decorating scheme better than a clear finish. Or it may be that the floor is so badly damaged, or made from such an inferior wood, that it is unsightly and would be best covered with paint.

It is possible to combine paint with traditional, clear-finish products on the same floor. Some professional designers decorate wood floors by stencilling a painted design on them. Another method of decoration is to paint a border round the edge of the floor and stain the rest.

**Preparing wood floors for finishing**  Whether you are going to paint or stain your wood floor, you must begin by making the necessary repairs. These preparations may include replacing wood plugs, fixing warped planks (*see p.114*) or removing and replacing damaged planks (*see p.115*). It may be necessary to sand a wood floor, especially if you intend to stain it or apply a clear finish to it (*see pp.116-117*). Before you sand the floor, countersink any protruding nail heads, using a hammer and nail punch. This will secure the planks and prevent the nails from ripping the sandpaper.

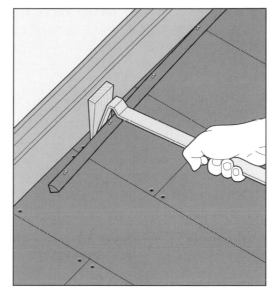

### Removing the beading
Some skirting boards may have a narrow strip of beading attached to the base. Removing this beading allows you to sand and apply finish right up to the edge of the floor. Gently prise off the beading with a crowbar. Wedge a thin piece of wood between the skirting board and the crow bar to protect the finish. When the beading is reinstalled, it will hide any rough edges around the perimeter of the room.

| FLOOR FINISHES | | | |
|---|---|---|---|
| **Type of finish** | **Colour** | **Drying time** | **Sheen** |
| Paint | Limited selection | Fast | Satin to gloss |
| Oil-based polyurethane | Amber when dry | Slow | Satin to gloss |
| Water-based acrylic | Clear | Fast | Satin to gloss |
| Seal and wax | Amber | Slow | Wax shine |

### BEADINGS
Some antique beadings have decorative finishes. Take care to avoid damaging them so that you can reuse them. Most softwood mouldings are relatively cheap to replace, so don't be upset if softwood beading splits during removal. It is more important to devote your time to protecting the finish on the skirting board.

## REPLACING WOOD PLUGS

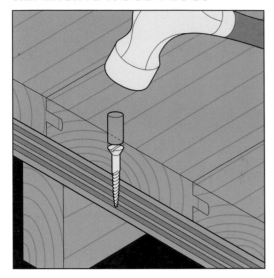

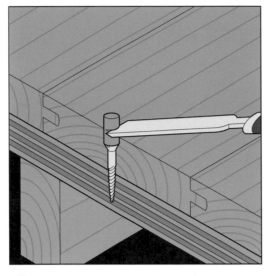

**1  Tap the dowels into holes**
Some floors have plugs that hide screw heads. If you cannot find replacements for missing plugs, use hard-wood dowels. Coat the sides of the dowels with glue and tap them into the holes.

**2  Cut the dowel**
When the glue has dried, use a chisel or a fine-toothed saw to cut the part of the dowel that is sticking up out of the floor. Sand the dowel level with the floor, then stain it to match.

## FIXING WARPED DECORATIVE BOARDS

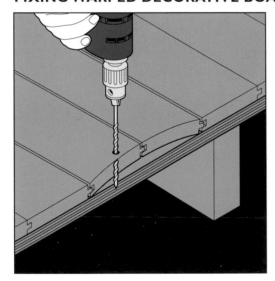

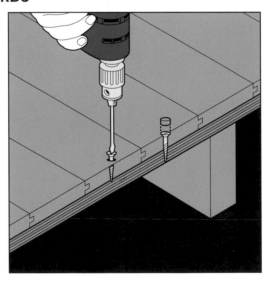

**1  Drill pilot holes**
Screw down warped decorative boards. Drill pilot holes, slightly smaller than the screws, every 7.5 or 10 cm (3 or 4in) along the warp. The screws should be 6.25mm (¼in) shorter than the thickness of the decorative board and floorboard.

**2  Screw back into position**
Drive wood screws into the holes. This will pull the board back. If more than one board is warped, work from the edges of the damaged area towards the centre. Hide the repair by countersinking the screws and covering them with wood plugs.

---

**PROFESSIONAL TIP**

Different woods absorb stains in different ways. If you cannot find plugs made from the same wood as your floor, you will need to find a stain formulation that will make the new plug match the floor precisely. Experiment with different formulations on a test piece of wood. Allow the stain to dry thoroughly before comparing colours.

**WORKING ON PLANKS FROM UNDERNEATH**

If you have a decorative planked floor laid over existing floorboards, you may find this the easiest way to fix warped boards. Place a weight, or have a helper stand, on the damaged area. Drill pilot holes and drive screws with metal washers through the floorboards into the wood boards. This should pull the wood back into its proper position.

## REMOVING DAMAGED BOARDS

### To remove a complete board
Remove a complete board that is damaged by splitting it with a wood chisel in a number of places. Then prise up the pieces. Remove nails with a claw hammer.

### To remove part of a board
To remove a damaged section of a large board, drill a series of holes at each end of the damaged area. Square the edges with a wood chisel. Replace the section of board.

## FIXING A SQUEAKY FLOOR

A squeaky floor is usually caused by one piece of wood rubbing against another. To silence the noise, the rubbing must be prevented. If the source of the problem is above a joist and you have access to the underside of the floor, apply carpenter's glue to a shim and drive it between the joist and the sub-floor. If you have to work from above, drill pilot holes and drive screws or annular nails into the joist or sub-floor. Tightening up the connections usually eliminates the rubbing.

## REPLACING A TONGUE-AND-GROOVE BOARD

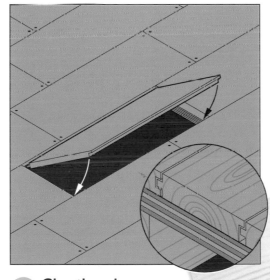

**1 Prepare the new board**
Cut the new board to the correct length to fill the gap. Turn the board upside down and remove the bottom lip of the groove with a chisel.

**2 Glue the edges**
Apply carpenter's glue to the edges of the tongue and the remaining part of the groove. Tip the section at an angle and insert the tongue into the groove of the adjoining plank.

### SANDING

If you are planning to repaint a floor, simply prepare the surface by scraping away any loose paint and cleaning the floor. However, if you plan to apply a new clear protective finish to a floor, you will need to sand away the existing finish first.

To sand a floor, you will need a drum sander, an edge sander, a rotary buffer and various hand-held scrapers. You can hire most of these tools – except for the scrapers – from a tool-hire shop. Describe the condition of the floor and its size to the shop assistant. He will advise you about the type of machines, abrasives and polishers that you will need. Ask the assistant to demonstrate how to use the machines. You will also need abrasive paper for the drum sander and edge sander, and wire wool or buffing pads for the rotary buffer.

Remember that a drum sander is a very powerful tool that can easily damage your floor if you are not careful. A rotary buffer can be difficult to use. Some have controls on the handle, others work when the handle is moved up and down, an action that may need some practice. It is important to keep moving, as buffing in one place for too long can remove too much of the finish.

**Using a drum sander**
Attach paper to the drum, following the dealer's directions. The key to using a drum sander is to ensure that you keep it moving when the sandpaper is in contact with the floor. Keep the sander in the up position when standing still and lower it as you move forwards or backwards.

### Sanding the floor

Begin at one end of the room with the sander loaded with a rough-grit sandpaper, and pointing in the direction in which the boards are laid. Always sand along the grain of the wood. Stand about two thirds of the way across the room. Turn the machine on with the sander raised off the floor, begin walking, and slowly lower the sander to the floor. As you get close to the opposite wall, raise the sander. Then walk backwards over the same strip, lowering the sander into position while moving.

As you near your original starting point, raise the sander. Move the machine 100 or 125mm (4 or 5in) to the side and begin a new pass. Continue sanding in this way until you reach the far end of the room. Then point the sander in the opposite direction and sand the remaining third of the floor in the same manner. When you have finished, switch to a finer-grit paper and begin the whole process again.

## SANDING DIFFICULT AREAS OF THE FLOOR

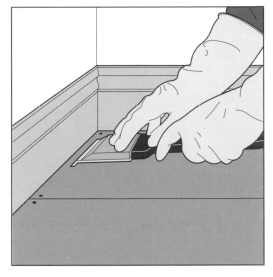

**1 Guide the sander back and forth**
Use an edge sander for areas against the wall. Where the floorboards are parallel to the wall, guide the tool back and forth in the direction of the wood grain. Start with a rough-grit disc for the first pass. Follow with finer-grit discs.

**2 Follow the grain of the wood**
Where the boards are at right angles to the wall, guide the edge sander against the skirting board and then pull away in a half circle motion. Overlap the area sanded by the drum sander by 100 to 125mm (4 to 5in).

**3 Sanding hard-to-reach areas**
Use the hand scraper to remove the finish from corners and other out-of-the-way areas. Pull the blade of the tool towards you. Follow by hand sanding with medium-grit and then fine-grit paper attached to a sanding block.

## SANDING PARQUET FLOORS

These floors present a special challenge because each parquet or floor tile is made up of a number of small pieces of wood set at right angles to each other. Special care must be taken to avoid leaving ugly cross-grain scratches on the surface when you sand.

To remove the finish from a parquet floor, sand in a diagonal pattern. Use a floor sander and attach a medium grit paper. Make the first pass starting in one corner and working to the opposite corner. Sand the entire floor in this direction. Switch to a finer paper and make the second pass on the opposite diagonal. Sand the entire floor. The final pass should be made parallel to the longest wall using a buffer equipped with a sanding disc.

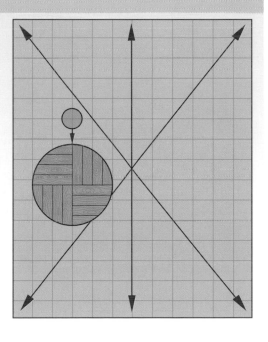

## SANDING SAFELY

Sanding produces wood dust that can be highly combustible. Power sanders have a bag which catch most of the wood dust, but some will escape, so wear a dust mask. Confine the dust to the room in which you are working, by hanging plastic dust sheets over all doorways, and sealing the edges with masking tape.

Learn when and how to empty the dust-collection bag. To be safe, store the dust in a metal tin until it can be disposed of.

Power sanders are noisy so you should wear earplugs.

## APPLYING THE FINISH TO A FLOOR

Apply a stain or clear finish immediately after sanding a floor. In this way you will avoid the possibility of the exposed wood becoming marked.

First of all, sweep and vacuum up all the dust, including that on window ledges and on the top of skirting boards. Any dust and dirt that becomes stuck to the wet finish will make the surface rough. Fill any nail holes or gouges in the floor with wood filler and then sand them level and remove any dust.

**Painting a wood floor** If you are removing a clear finish, sand (*see p.116*), then sweep and vacuum up any dust. Apply either a solvent-based or a water-based primer to the floor, then use either a solvent-based or water-based floor paint for the final coats.

**Painting a concrete floor** Although a concrete floor does not require sanding, it should be cleaned thoroughly and any cracks and dents should be filled with patching concrete. (You can buy bags of pre-mixed patching concrete at DIY centres and hardware shops.) Follow this by priming and sealing the concrete with a masonry primer, then finish with paint that is specially made for concrete floors.

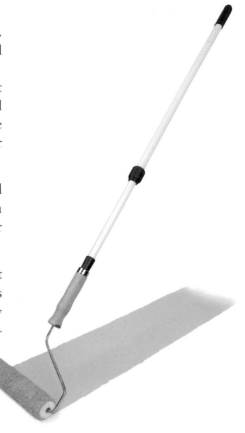

## STAINING AND SEALING FLOORS

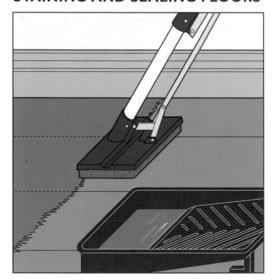

**1 Applying wood stain**
Use a roller, brush or foam pad to apply the stain. Begin in the corner farthest from the door and apply stain to a large, square area. Once the stain has seeped into the wood (*see p.87*), wipe it up with a clean cloth. Allow the stain to dry.

**2 Applying a clear finish**
If you are finishing with a solvent-based polyurethane, first buff the floor with a rotary buffing machine using fine wire wool. If finishing with a water-based varnish, use a buffing screen. Apply the finish round the perimeter of the floor with a clean brush.

**3 Apply at least two coats**
Over the rest of the floor, follow the grain of the wood and apply the finish with a brush or a lamb's-wool applicator. Buff with fine abrasives between each coat and clean up any dust. For good protection you should apply at least two coats of finish.

## PAINTING WOOD FLOORS

### 1 Paint along the edge

Always start painting a floor in the corner farthest from the door. Use a 75mm (3in) brush to paint a neat edge on the floor close to each wall. Paint a strip about 1.5m (5 feet) along each wall.

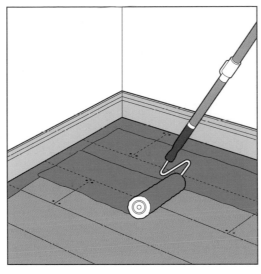

### 2 Paint along the boards

Use a roller and a roller extension. Lay on the paint in the direction of the floorboards within the border you have just painted. Make sure that the roller head contains enough paint.

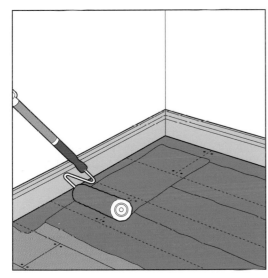

### 3 Paint across the boards

To make sure that the section is completely covered with paint, without reloading the roller, paint across the boards, back over the area that you have just painted.

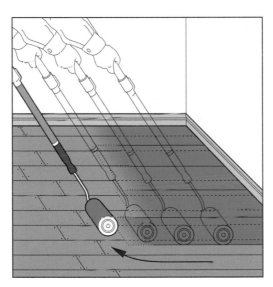

### 4 Paint the rest of the floor

Finish painting the entire floor by rolling paint along the wood grain. Feather the edges of each section. Work across the narrowest part of the room first, but be careful not to paint yourself into a corner.

### PROFESSIONAL TIP

Painting floors is usually extremely uncomfortable if you have to work bending over and kneeling down. You can minimise bending by using a roller extension. You will have to kneel to paint the edges with a brush. Wear knee pads (you can buy them in sports shops or garden centres), or kneel on an old piece of carpet or rigid-foam insulation board.

### PAINTING CONCRETE FLOORS

### Lay on in a zig-zag pattern

Start in the corner farthest from the door and work in manageable sections. Lay on the paint in a zig-zag pattern and then roll in a perpendicular direction for complete coverage across each section.

# Metal pipes and radiators

Many older houses have exposed metal pipes and radiators that can be painted to match the rest of the room. The main difference between painting metal and painting wood surfaces is in the type of paint you use. Although most paint that is used for walls and woodwork can be used on metal too, it is best to use paints that are specially formulated for the purpose. These contain rust inhibitors and will protect the metal if it is exposed to water due to a leak or condensation. Buy paint with a label that states that it contains a rust inhibitor, and is suitable for metal.

**Dealing with hot pipes** Turn off the hot water supply when you are painting water pipes and turn off the central heating when working on heating pipes and radiators. Wait for the paint to dry thoroughly before turning the water or heating back on.

**Painting pipes** If the pipe butts up against a wall, mask the wall to protect it. Spread a dust sheet on the floor under the pipe. You can use one dust sheet and move it along as you progress down the length of the pipe.

**MATERIALS AND TOOLS**

**Metal primers**
**Metal paints**
**Stiff brushes**
**Rollers and brushes (special shapes may be required for irregular sufaces)**
**Dust sheets**
**Paint mitt (optional)**
**Scouring pads**
**Paint sprayer (optional)**
**Wire wool**

## PREPARING AND PAINTING PIPES

**1 Prepare the pipe**
Remove loose paint from a metal pipe with a stiff brush or wire wool. Avoid shaking the pipe loose from its mounting bracket by holding the pipe with one hand and brushing it with the other. Wipe the pipe with a damp cloth.

**2 Lay the paint on the pipe**
The pipe's size will determine which brush to use. Lay on the paint round the circumference of a small section of the pipe. Without reloading, smooth the paint down the length of the section. Move the dust sheet and continue on the next section.

## USING A PAINTER'S MITT

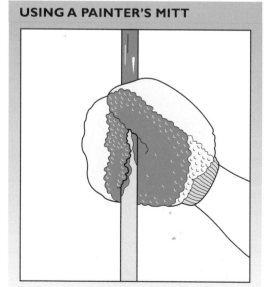

Dip the palm of the mitt in a paint tray and blot it on the sloping area of the tray. Grasp the pipe between the thumb and the rest of the mitt and slide the mitt along the pipe. Go back and forth along the pipe a few times to ensure even coverage.

## RADIATORS

Radiators present two main problems: they have hard-to-reach areas and, because they are usually set close to the wall, it is difficult to paint the back of the radiator and the wall.

**Cleaning radiators** Make sure that the heating is switched off and that the radiator is cool. Clean the radiator with warm, soapy water to remove any dirt and grease. To remove stubborn stains, scour with a scouring pad. Rinse the radiator and allow it to dry thoroughly.

**Painting radiators** Protect the floor under the radiator with a dust sheet. If you need to protect the wall behind the radiator, tape a dust sheet or a plastic sheet onto the wall. Apply a water-based metal paint to the radiator if you wish to turn on the heating soon after painting it. The combination of solvent-based paint and heat can produce unpleasant fumes until the paint dries completely. Paint radiators with a brush or a paint sprayer, and make sure that they are covered completely. Cover the radiator air vent before painting. The vent allows air to escape from the heating system, and it will malfunction if it is painted over.

## PREPARING AND PAINTING RADIATORS

**1  Preparing the radiator**
Use a stiff brush to remove loose paint. Then, using a long-handled brush for hard-to-reach areas, apply a metal primer to any bare spots.

**2  Painting the radiator**
You may need to use several different-sized brushes to paint a radiator. There are pads and mini rollers on flexible handles that help you to reach areas inaccessible to brushes, rollers and pads on rigid handles.

**USING A PAINT SPRAYER**

Keep the tip of the paint sprayer at right angles to the radiator as you move it from side to side. Protect the floor, and the walls near the radiator by covering them with newspaper or cardboard.

# Masonry surfaces

Although they are usually left unfinished, all brick, concrete-block and poured-concrete surfaces may be painted. Primers designed for masonry seal the porous surfaces of these materials and provide a good base for the masonry paint.

**Preparing masonry** Thorough preparation is essential. Dirt and grease should be removed with household detergent. If mildew is present, coat it with a solution of 0.57 litres (1 pint) of chlorine bleach to 1.7 litres (3 pints) of water. Leave for 24 hours, rinse off and allow to dry.

Repair the walls by filling cracks. It may be necessary to replace mortar, a process known as repointing. Tackle only small repairs yourself; extensive repointing is best left to a professional. Make sure that you use the right type of mortar, because modern mortar may damage old masonry. If you are in doubt about what to use, ask a professional who has worked on similar buildings.

**Using a high-pressure water sprayer** Clean the entire wall, including grout and mortar joints, with a high-pressure water sprayer. Ask at your tool-hire shop or DIY centre for instructions about how to use it. The sprayer will remove dirt and loose paint.

| MATERIALS AND TOOLS |
| --- |
| **Masonry primer** |
| **Masonry paint** |
| **Cleaning solutions** |
| **Stiff brush** |
| **Patching concrete or mortar** |
| **Trowel** |
| **Wire wool** |
| **Hammer and chisel** |
| **Pointing tool** |
| **Mortar board** |
| **Brushes and rollers** |
| **Waterproofing compound** |
| **High-pressure water sprayer** |

## DEALING WITH EFFLORESCENCE

Efflorescence is a chalky, powdery residue that forms when salts dry out on the masonry. It will prevent paint from bonding to the surface properly, and will cause it to peel a short time after it is applied. It is therefore essential that all traces of efflorescence are removed before painting.

To remove efflorescence, brush it off with a dry, stiff-bristled brush. Remove all traces of dust by wiping the surface with a damp cloth.

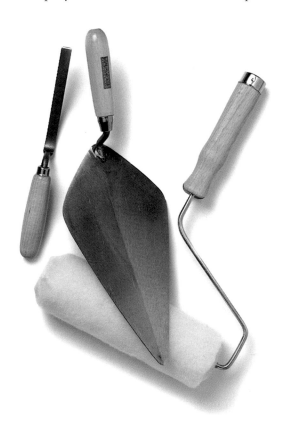

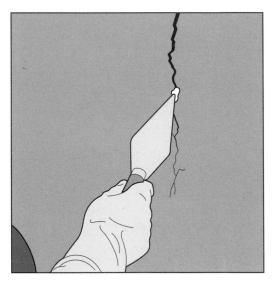

**Patching a concrete wall**
Use patching mortar to fill cracks in concrete walls. Mix the mortar according to the directions on the packet and apply it with a trowel. Allow the area to dry and then rub it with a wire brush.

## REPAIRING AND PAINTING MORTAR AND MASONRY

**1 Remove crumbling mortar**
Use a hammer and a cold chisel to remove crumbling mortar to a depth of about 12.5mm (1/2in). Wear safety glasses when removing mortar.

**2 Brush out the joint**
Clean out the joint with a stiff brush, taking care to remove all of the loose mortar. Mix enough new mortar to make the repair and put it onto a small board.

**3 Mortar the open joint**
Using a trowel, transfer some mortar from the board into the open joint. Make sure that the joint is filled completely, but do not overfill it. Use a pointing tool to smooth the mortar. Use a stiff brush to remove mortar from the face of the brick.

**4 Apply the paint to the surface**
Use a long-nap roller to apply paint to masonry surfaces. Lay the paint on in zig-zags and then roll in the opposite direction, for even coverage. Finish with vertical strokes, then proceed to the next section of the wall.

### DAMPPROOFING CELLAR WALLS

Minor water-seepage problems in cellar walls can be eliminated by applying a waterproofing compound. Prepare the walls, then brush on waterproofing compound as directed on the label, and allow to dry. Some cement-based products will require a few days to cure properly. It is important that the first coat is completely dry before you apply a second. Waterproofing compounds can usually be covered with water-based paint.

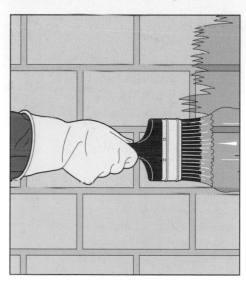

**Apply waterproofing compound**
Apply waterproofing compound with a large, synthetic-bristle brush. Jab and pack the compound into all the joints and cracks. Allow to dry before recoating.

Cleaning and storing equipment and materials properly is an important part of a painting job. If you have bought good-quality tools, following the cleaning procedures outlined in this chapter will help to prolong their life. You will also learn how to dispose of hazardous materials and how to store paints and solvents safely.

# CHAPTER 9

# CLEANING, CARE AND MAINTENANCE

# Cleaning up

The steps you take to clean up will depend on which stage of the painting project you have reached. The procedure for cleaning tools each day during a painting project is not the same as the procedure for cleaning up after you have completed the work.

**During a painting project** If you plan to continue work the next day, there is no need to store tools and materials. Just make sure that you pour the paint from paint kettles and roller trays back into the tin. Then replace the lid and put the paint tin out of reach of children, but close to where you will be working the next day. If you plan to use the room in the meantime, roll up the dust sheets, otherwise they will be pushed out of position by normal foot traffic. You can leave masking tape on windows and woodwork overnight. Place brushes and rollers in plastic bags *(see p.126)*. Try to keep your equipment in a convenient place and to leave the room as ready as possible for you to continue.

**After a painting project** When you have finished the project, cleaning should be much more thorough. An important part of the final cleaning process is putting the room back in order. Replace switch and socket plates and light fittings. Remove any masking tape that is still in place. If you used water-based paint, it should be dry enough to remove the tape from window panes a day after painting. When cleaning brushes and other small items, it is best to work at a large sink. If you don't have a large sink, use a large bucket. After you have removed the paint from brushes and rollers, allow the water to run for a few minutes to clear the drain of paint.

**MATERIALS AND TOOLS**

**Buckets**
**Newspaper**
**Solvents**
**Rubber gloves**

## CLEANING AND STORING BRUSHES

With proper maintenance, a good-quality brush will last for years. The secret is to remove all the paint from it after use. Start cleaning by working the brush across an old newspaper to remove most of the paint. Then treat the brushes with the appropriate solvent. For water-based paints, hold the brush under a stream of running water. Use white spirit for oil-based paints. Help the solvent to reach deep into the bristles by flexing them so that they fan out. Remove the solvent by washing the brush in hot, soapy water. Dry the brush thoroughly and wrap the bristles before storing (*see p.127*). For long-term storage, hang the brush up so that the bristles do not support its weight.

## CLEANING AND STORING ROLLER SLEEVES

A roller sleeve can soak up a lot of paint during the course of a project. Not only will it become saturated, paint also seems to work its way inside it. To clean a roller sleeve, you will need to use white spirit to remove oil-based paint. You may be able to remove water-based paint with your hand, while holding the sleeve under running water.

### REMOVING PAINT FROM TOOLS AND YOURSELF

You may need to remove paint from the tools and yourself. Use a rag dipped in solvent to remove paint from tools. Make sure that they are thoroughly dry before you store them.

Soap and water will remove water-based paint from your skin. Shampoo should remove paint from your hair, but if not, comb the paint out when it is dry.

Remove oil-based paint from your skin with a rag dipped in white spirit. Make sure that you wash with warm soapy water after applying this solvent, as it may irritate your skin.

## CLEANING AND DRYING BRUSHES

**1 Remove the paint**
Pour the appropriate solvent into a clean bucket. Wearing rubber gloves, put the brush in the solvent and rub the paint off the bristles; you may need a brush-cleaning comb. Clean paint off the handle and ferrule with a rag dipped in solvent.

**2 Dry the brush**
Wipe the cleaned and rinsed brush on newspaper. Then shake it well to remove excess solvent. You can do this by hand or with a spinning tool. In either case, be sure to spin the brush so that the spray lands inside a bucket or waste bin.

### PROFESSIONAL TIP

Don't bother cleaning brushes or rollers if you plan to continue the project the next day. Use the professional's time-saving trick of placing the equipment in plastic bags while it is still wet. The plastic will keep the paint damp overnight. The following day, simply make a few practice passes before you begin. (*See Chapter 2, p.27, for advice on how to refurbish brushes.*)

## WRAPPING AND STORING BRUSHES

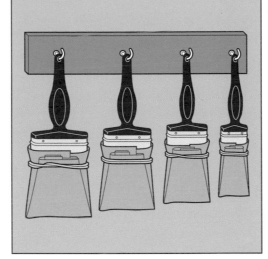

**1 Wrap the brushes**
When the brushes are clean and dry, wrap them in kitchen paper so that the bristles remain straight. Secure the paper with a rubber band or tie it with string.

**2 Store brushes properly**
Store brushes by hanging them on hooks with their bristles downwards. You may have to drill holes in the handles. If you are storing a number of brushes, label each wrapper with the size of the brush.

## CLEANING AND STORING ROLLERS

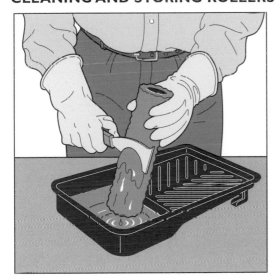

**1 Clean rollers with solvent**
Pour solvent into a clean roller tray and submerge the roller sleeve. Wear rubber gloves and use a 5-in-1 tool to rub the paint out of the sleeve. When the sleeve is clean, squeeze it out and rinse it in clean solvent. Stand the sleeve on end to dry.

**2 Wrap rollers for storage**
Wrap the rollers loosely in plastic, or kitchen paper. Secure the wrapper by twisting the edges.

### REUSING TOOLS

You can reuse tools any number of times until they simply don't work any more. Try a few practice passes with an old roller or brush before you begin painting with it. If it leaves brush or roller marks, or if it does not hold or dispense the paint smoothly, buy a new one.

If you unwrap a brush and there are still traces of paint on the bristles, or if the bristles come free when you give them a light tug, get rid of the brush. Many professional painters use new sleeves for each project.

### CLEANING PAINT KETTLES

Clean paint kettles by first pouring and brushing as much paint as possible back into the paint tin. Then use the kettle to clean the brushes and other tools. Pour in solvent and use a brush to remove paint from the sides and bottom. Then clean the brush. Finally, rinse out the kettle and dry it with a clean cloth.

## STORING PAINT

Paint that is sealed in its tin and stored properly will keep for many years and, after a little stirring, will be ready to use. At the end of a project, pour all the leftover paint of the same type and colour into as few tins as possible. If you can no longer read the label, write the colour and sheen on a label and stick it on the lid.

Most paint labels provide information on storage. In general, the paint should be stored in an area where it will not freeze and where children and pets can't reach it. A lockable paint-storage cabinet (see p.53) is the best place.

**Disposing of paint** Small amounts of water-based paint that are left over at the end of your painting project can simply be left in the tin, sealed carefully and placed in the dustbin.

Oil-based paint is a hazardous substance, it must not be thrown in a dustbin. Make enquiries at your local council about how to dispose of the paint. Never pour old paint down the drain.

**Disposing of solvents** The solvents used for oil-based paints are hazardous and should be stored out of the reach of children. It is a good idea to recycle solvents for future use.

**Seal the paint tin**
Remove paint from the groove on the lip of the tin with a brush or rag. Place the original lid in position. Protect the lid with a rag and use a hammer to seal the tin.

## RECYCLING SOLVENTS

**1  Pour solvent into a container**
Pour the used solvent into a clean container that has a lid. You may need to use a funnel. Seal the lid tightly and leave for a few days to allow the paint particles to settle at the bottom of the container.

**2  Decant the re-usable solvent**
When the used solvent has separated out, the clear, reusable liquid will settle over the paint particles. Strain the clear liquid into another container that has a lid, and save it for another painting project.

**3  Dispose of the solvent residue**
Add cat litter, sawdust or any other absorbent material to the water-based paint residue in the first container and place in a dustbin. Call your local council for information on how to dispose of large volumes of unwanted solvents.

# Care and maintenance

Regular cleaning will keep painted finishes looking like new. Surfaces with glossy sheens can be cleaned with soap and water, but duller surfaces should be dusted. Clean spots from matt or eggshell finishes on walls and ceilings with warm water. If that does not work, consult the manufacturer for instructions.

Keep a record of your painting jobs and the paint manufacturers' phone numbers so that you can get in touch with them, if necessary. The record should also tell you the exact shade used during the project, how much paint the job required and how long it took to do the job. This information will be valuable when you decide to repaint the room.

**Paint touch ups** Repair nicks and chips in a paint finish by touching them up with the original paint. Use as small a brush as possible to apply the paint. If the touch up dries to a different colour from the original paint, you may have to repaint an entire section of surface. For example, if you make a repair, it may be necessary to repaint part of the wall or a section of woodwork so that the repair does not stand out.

**Maintaining floors** Use a mop, or a vacuum cleaner with a wood floor attachment to keep the surface of hard floors free of dirt. To remove stains, use a cleaner appropriate to the surface finish. Restore the shine by buffing the surface with a lamb's wool pad.

When buffing no longer revives the shine, apply a new coat of finish. For polyurethanes, clean the floor and dull the existing finish with wire wool, a sanding screen or sandpaper. Remove the dust, then apply the new finish in thin coats *(see p.118)*. Allow each coat to dry before re-coating.

## PAINTING LOG

Here's what to keep for future reference:

- Dates of the paint project.
- Colour samples and sheens for each room.
- How long the project took to complete.
- A record of the amount of paint you used, the number of coats you applied, and any repairs you performed before painting.
- Manufacturers' phone numbers.
- All receipts.

## PLASTIC TIN LIDS

You can buy sometimes buy plastic covers for sealing open tins. Not only do they fit securely but they can be reused. It is still necessary to remove paint from the tin lip before sealing.

## DISPOSING OF OLD PAINT TINS

Paint tins that are made from steel can be flattened down for easier disposal. Make sure you dispose of the paint safely *(p.128)*.

Quantities of paint must never be poured down the drain – contact your local council for information on what you should do.

# Glossary

**BALUSTER**
The vertical posts which support the handrail of a staircase.

**BALUSTRADE**
The handrail, baluster and newel posts on a staircase.

**BOXING**
Mixing together tins of paint of the same shade, to ensure a uniform colour throughout.

**BRUSH COMB**
A plastic or metal tool used to remove paint from a brush.

**CHEMICAL STRIPPER**
A liquid, paste or gel which is used to remove paint from a surface.

**CHINA BRISTLE BRUSH**
A high-quality brush containing natural bristles including boar's hair.

**COLOUR WHEEL**
A design device which shows the relationship between primary, secondary and tertiary colours.

**COMPLEMENTARY COLOURS**
Colours which lie directly opposite each other on the colour wheel.

**COOL COLOURS**
Colours containing elements of blue or green.

**CORNICE**
Moulding fitted at the junction between a wall and ceiling.

**CUTTING IN**
Using a paintbrush to paint a wall where it meets the ceiling or woodwork. Cutting in ensures coverage at the edges of walls or ceilings that are painted with a roller.

**DADO RAIL**
Decorative moulding that divides the lower one-third of a wall from the upper two-thirds.

**DECORATIVE FINISH**
Any painted surface with an unusual design where the paint does not appear as a solid colour.

**DRAGGING**
A decorative paint finish which is achieved by pulling a brush through paint that has just been applied and is still wet.

**DUST MASK**
A paper mask worn over the nose and mouth to prevent the wearer from breathing in large particles of dust and dirt.

**EFFLORESCENCE**
A chalky, powdery residue caused by salts which leach out of masonry and dry on the surface.

**EGGSHELL**
An intermediate and less intense level of sheen or glossiness in paint.

**EMULSION PAINT**
A broad term for water-based paints containing vinyl or acrylic resins.

**FEATHERING**
Brushing with the tips of the bristles on a brush; or touching lightly with a roller to blend two areas of paint without leaving visible lap marks.

**JOINT COMPOUND**
Plaster-based material used to fill joints between sheets of plasterboard, and to make repairs in damaged plasterboard.

**LEAD PAINT**
Paint containing a high percentage of lead. As lead has been banned from use in paint you will only come across it when removing layers of old paint (*see p.53*).

**LINING PAPER**
Smooth, unpatterned wallpaper used to cover cracks and other imperfections in walls.

**MASKING TAPE**
Tape designed to protect areas adjacent to surfaces which are being painted.

**PAINT PAD**
A synthetic, sponge-like pad connected to a plastic handle and used instead of a brush.

**PLASTER**
A mixture of lime, sand and water applied in layers to the surface of a wall or ceiling.

**PLASTERBOARD**
Building material which consists of a gypsum core and paper facing.

**PLATFORM**
Construction consisting of a plank supported between two ladders or trestles and used to gain access to high areas.

**PLUMB LINE**
Device consisting of a line with a weight attached to one end, used to find the true vertical.

**POLYURETHANE VARNISH**
Easily applied, durable, transparent matt or gloss finish for wood.

**RAGGING**
A decorative finish which is achieved by applying paint with a rag.

**RELATED COLOURS**
Colours which are located next to one another on the colour wheel.

**RESPIRATOR**
Mask which screens out very small dust particles and purifies air as it is inhaled.

**SHEEN**
The level of glossiness of a paint when it is dry.

**SOLVENTS**
Liquids which break down or dissolve other materials. They are used in paints, cleaning materials and paint strippers.

**SPONGING**
A decorative finish which is achieved by dabbing paint or glaze onto a surface with a sponge.

**SUGAR SOAP**
A highly concentrated compound for cleaning and stripping paint, which leaves no soapy residue.

**TEXTURED PAINTS**
Paint which contains additives which cause it to dry to a rough or textured finish.

**THINNING**
Adding solvent to paint so that it flows more easily.

**VOLATILE ORGANIC COMPOUND (VOC)**
Hazardous carbon-based chemical additive in oil-based paint.

**WALL FILLER**
Plaster-based material used to make repairs in plasterboard and plaster. It is available in dry powder form, or ready-mixed.

**WARM COLOURS**
Colours containing elements of yellow or red.

**WET EDGE**
An area to which paint has just been applied, but which has not yet begun to dry.

**WOOD FILLER**
Material which may contain synthetic resins, used to make repairs in wood.

**WOOD STAIN**
A transparent finish which colours wood but allows the grain to show through.

# Suppliers

### Retailers with branches nationwide

**B & Q plc**
1 Hampshire Corporate Park
Chandlers Ford
Eastleigh
Hampshire SO5 3YX
01703 – 256 256

**C Brewer & Sons Ltd**
Albany House
Ashford Road
Eastbourne
East Sussex BN21 3TR
01323 – 411 080

**Do It All**
Falcon House
The Minories
Dudley
West Midlands DY2 8PG
01384 – 456 456

**FADS (A G Stanley)**
Victoria Mills
Macclesfield Road
Holmes Chapel
Cheshire CW4 7JB
01477 – 544 544

**Great Mills (Retail)**
RMC House
Paulton
Bristol BS18 5SX
01761 – 416 034

**Homebase *and* Texas Homecare**
Beddington House
Railway Approach
Wallington
Surrey SM6 0HB
0181 – 784 7200

**Wickes Building Supplies**
120–138 Station Road
Harrow
Middlesex HA1 2QB
0181 – 901 2000

**Woolworths plc**
Woolworth House
242–246 Marylebone Road
London NW1 6JL
0171 – 262 1222
(Suppliers of Cover Plus paint)

### Paint, varnish and wood stain manufacturers

**Blackfriars' paints, varnishes and stains: see E Parsons & Sons Ltd**

**J W Bollom & Co Ltd**
PO Box 78
Croydon Road
Beckenham
Kent BR3 4BL
0181 – 658 2299
(Makers of Bromel and Flameguard paints)

**Bromel paint: see J W Bollom & Co Ltd**

**Cementone Beaver Ltd**
Tingewick Road
Buckingham
Buckinghamshire MK18 1AN
01280 – 828 823

**Coo-Var Ltd**
Ellenshaw Works
Lockwood Street
Hull
North Humberside HU2 0HN
01482 – 328 053

**Crown Berger Ltd**
Crown House
Hollins Road
Darwen
Lancashire BB3 0BG
01254 – 704 951
(Makers of Crown and Magicote paints)

**Cuprinol Ltd**
Adderwell
Frome
Somerset BA11 1NL
01373 – 465 151

**Dulux paint: see ICI Paints Division**

**Flameguard paint: see J W Bollom & Co Ltd**

**Hammerite Products Ltd**
Prudhoe
Northumberland NE42 6LP
01661 – 830 000

**Humbrol Ltd**
Marfleet
Hull
North Humberside HU9 5NE
01482 – 701 191

**ICI Paints Division**
Wexham Road
Slough
Berkshire SL2 5DS
01753 – 550 000
(Makers of Dulux paint)

**International Paint Retail Division**
24–30 Canute Road
Southampton
Hampshire SO9 3AS
01703 – 226 722

**Johnstone's paints: see Kalon Decorative Products**

**Kalon Decorative Products**
Huddersfield Road
Birstall
West Yorkshire WF17 9XA
01924 – 477 201
(Makers of Johnstone's and Leyland paints)

**John T Keep & Sons Ltd: see J W Bollom & Co Ltd**

**Leyland paint: see Kalon Decorative Products Ltd**

**Magicote paint: see Crown Berger Ltd**

**E Parsons & Sons Ltd**
Blackfriars Road
Nailsea
Bristol
Avon BS19 2DJ
01275 – 854 911
(Makers of Blackfriars' paints, varnishes and stains)

**J & H Ratcliff & Co (Paints) Ltd**
135a Linaker Street
Stockport
Merseyside PR8 5DF
01704 – 537 999

**Rustins Ltd**
Waterloo Road
Cricklewood
London NW2 7TX
0181 – 450 4666

**Arthur Sanderson & Sons Ltd**
100 Acres
Sanderson Road
Uxbridge
Middlesex UB8 1DH
01895 – 238 244
(Makers of Sanderson Spectrum paint)

# Index

**AUTHOR'S ACKNOWLEDGMENTS**

Many paint manufacturers and professional associations that serve the industry provide valuable information for the do-it-yourself painter. Some useful suppliers' addresses are listed on page 132. The professional associations that we wish to thank include Benjamin Moore & Company USA, Sherwin-Williams Company USA, the Rohm and Haas Paint Quality Institute USA and the National Paint and Coatings Association USA for their kind help.


**PUBLISHER'S ACKNOWLEDGMENTS**

The publishers of this book wish to thank:–

Leyland Paint Stockists
335–337 Kings Road
London SW3 5EU

Crucial Trading
4 St. Barnabas Street
Pimlico Green
London SW1
(for supplying floor covering)


**Photographic credits:**

Werner Ladders, USA p.32, p.55

Hiretech, Hire Technician's Group Ltd, UK p.116

Geoff Dann: p.1, pp.2–3, pp.4–5, pp.8–9, p.18, pp.20–21, pp.22–31, pp.34–35, p.37, p.40, pp.42–48, pp.51–52, p.54, pp.56–58, p.60, p.63, p71, pp.75–80, p.82, p.88, p.95, pp.98–102, p.105, pp.108–109, p.115, p.118, pp.121–122, pp.124–125

Tim Imrie: p.11, pp.12–16

Matthew Ward: p.59